Chatsworth and Grey Bruce Ontario in Colour Photos, Saving Our History One Photo at a Time

Photography
by Barbara Raué
2018

Series Name: Cruising Ontario

Book 198: Chatsworth, Desboro, Dornoch, Wiliamsford, Keady, Duncan, Elmwood, Euphrasia, Dobbinton, Tara, Williscroft, Markdale

Cover photo: Williamsford, Page 35

Series Name: Cruising Ontario
Saving Our History One Photo at a Time
in colour photos

Towns in Alphabetical Order:
Aberfoyle, Acton, Alton, Amherstburg, Ancaster, Arthur, Auburn, Aylmer, Ayr, Beaver Valley, Belgrave, Belleville, Bloomingdale, Blyth, Brantford, Brockville, Burford, Burlington, Caledon, Caledonia, Cambridge, Carlow, Chatsworth, Clifford, Collingwood, Conestogo, Delhi, Dorchester to Aylmer, Drayton, Drumbo, Dundas, Dunlop, Eden Mills, Elmira, Elora, Erin, Essex, Fergus, Goderich, Grimsby, Guelph, Hagersville, Hamilton, Hanover, Harriston, Hespeler, Jarvis, Kingston, Kingsville, Kitchener, Lake Superior, Lincoln, Linwood, Listowel, London, Lucknow, Merrickville, Mono, Mount Forest, Mount Pleasant, Neustadt, New Hamburg, Newboro, Newport, Niagara-on-the-Lake, Oakville, Onondaga, Orangeville, Orillia, Owen Sound, Palmerston, Paris, Pelham, Perth, Peterborough, Petrolia, Port Colborne, Port Elgin, Portland, Preston, Rockwood, Sarnia, Sault Ste. Marie, Seaforth, Sheffield, Shelburne, Simcoe, Smiths Falls, Smithville, Southampton, St. Catharines, St. George, St. Jacobs, St. Marys, St. Thomas, Stoney Creek, Stratford, Thamesford, Thunder Bay, Tillsonburg, Toronto, Waterdown, Waterford, Waterloo, Welland, Wellesley, Westport, Windsor, Wingham, Woodstock

Book 196: Pelham
Book 197: Beaver Valley
Book 198: Chatsworth
Book 199: Wingham

Other Books by Barbara Raue

Coins of Gold

Arrows, Indians and Love

The Life and Times of Barbara

The Cromwell Family Book

Laura Secord Discovered

Daddy Where Are You?

Montana Series
Book 1: Montana Dream
Book 2: Life on the Montana Frontier
Book 3: Montana to Boston and Back
Book 4: Montana Sons Go to War
Book 5: Montana Sons Return From War

Visit Barbara's website to view all of her books
http://barbararaue.ca

© 2018 by Barbara Raue - All the photos in this book have been taken with my cameras. I own the rights to them.

Table of Contents

Chatsworth	Page 11
Desboro	Page 17
Dornoch	Page 29
Grey Road 40 and Grey Road 3	Page 31
Williamsford	Page 34
Marmion	Page 36
Keady	Page 37
Elmwood	Page 37
Duncan	Page 41
Euphrasia	Page 42
Markdale	Page 42
Arkwright	Page 49
Dobbinton	Page 52
Tara	Page 56
Williscroft	Page 62
Architectural Terms	Page 66
Building Styles	Page 69

Chatsworth is a township in south-western Ontario in Grey County located at the headwaters of the Styx, Saugeen, Sauble, Bighead, Spey, and the old Sydenham Rivers. The current township was formed on January 1, 2001 with the amalgamation of Holland Township, Sullivan Township, and the village of Chatsworth. The first white settlers arrived in this area in the early nineteenth century.

Canadian suffragette and activist Nellie McClung was born in the town of Chatsworth. The Sullivan Township area has a large Amish population.

The township includes the **town of Chatsworth**, Arnott, Berkeley, **Desboro, Dornoch**, Glascott, Grimston, Harkaway, Hemstock Mill, Holford, Holland Centre, **Keady**, Keward, Kinghurst, Lily Oak, Lueck Mill, Marmion, Massie, Mooresburg, Mount Pleasant, Peabody, Scone, Strathaven, Walters Falls, Williams Lake, and **Williamsford**.

Chatsworth is located south of Owen Sound and north of Durham where Highways 6 and 10 merge. The village neighbours Williamsford, Dornoch, and Desboro. Originally named *Johnstown* after an early landowner, the post office was renamed *Holland East* in 1851. It was renamed again to its present name in 1857. The name comes from Chatsworth House in Derbyshire, England near the home town of the postmaster at that time. Chatsworth was founded in 1848 at the northern terminus of the Toronto-Sydenham Colonization Road. Modern Highway 10 follows most of the original road's route.

The first building in the village of Desboro in 1856 was a log school house. The area was originally called Brown's Corners. At some point its name was changed to Donnybrook and then to Desborough after a village in central England. The first house and store were built in 1866 by George Smith. The Desboro hotel was built in 1869 and was one of the only rural taverns still operating in the township before it closed in 2011. The town hall was built in 1875 and enlarged to a two-storey building in 1950. Desboro is about 13 kilometers west of Chatsworth and Williamsford.

Keady is a small farming village, located at the intersection of Grey Roads 3 and 16. Keady saw its first settlers in the 1850s. The original general store was built in the late 1860s and operated for almost 100 years before being converted into a residence. It has a Community Centre, licensed mechanic, livestock market, machine shop and a United Church, and is home to about 200 people.

Keady is well known in the area for the weekly summer farmer's market and numerous functions held at the Keady Community Centre.

The village of Dornoch was settled by Bartholomew Griffin in 1841 when he encountered a crossroads that appealed to him. The area was originally called "Griffin's Corners" after Griffin started the first general store. In the late 1850s the village was served by a stage coach that was running between Durham and Chatsworth. Around the turn of the century, the name was changed to Dornoch after the village in northern Scotland. The community centre was built in 1952 and still serves Dornoch. Dornoch is situated between Williamsford and Durham on Highway 6 and is 33 kilometers south of Owen Sound.

Williamsford is a village on the North Saugeen River. It has a general store, post office, a bookstore and restaurant housed in a historic grain mill. A small dam controls the river. It has several churches, and a community cemetery. It is located on Highway 6 between Durham and Owen Sound. The village of Williamsford was first surveyed in 1858 comprising 400 acres in preparation for a railway which was to run from Toronto to Owen Sound. Each township was to contribute $40,000 to its construction. The post office was built in 1847 and the general store was built in the late 1800s. At the south end of the village sit the community centre grounds with a playground, a baseball diamond and a curling rink. The curling rink was completed in 2010 and has a lounge and two rinks. The community was previously served by a hockey arena with the original attached curling rink. The arena was planned in 1954 and opened officially in 1956 but was torn down in 2008.

West Grey is a township in western Ontario in Grey County spanning across the River Styx, the Rocky Saugeen River, the Beatty Saugeen River, and the South Saugeen River. Unlike most rural communities, West Grey maintains its own police force, the West Grey Police Service. The municipality was formed on January 1, 2001, when the former Townships of Bentinck, Glenelg, and Normanby, the Village of Neustadt, and the Town of Durham were amalgamated in a county-wide reorganization. Elmwood is one of the communities in this township.

Elmwood is a village in Grey County on the county line between Bruce and Grey, about six miles (10 kilometers) north of Hanover. It was a location in which Mennonites were to be found from before 1870, when ministers from Waterloo County were sent to Brant Township every eight weeks to conduct services which alternated in the homes of Mennonite families living there. In 1875, when the Mennonite Brethren in Christ (MBC) were organized in Ontario, Elmwood was one of their earliest places of worship. It was the village into which the retired farmers moved when they left the farms in that community. The MBCs first worshiped in private homes in the village and then in the United Brethren Church. As the United Brethren group lost out and the Mennonite Brethren in Christ grew in strength, the United Brethren church building was taken over by the MBC group, whose work continued well into the present century. Then as Mennonite young people were attracted away from their homes, the Mennonite Brethren in Christ membership decreased, until only a few members remained. In 1948 the church building was sold.

Duncan is located south of Thornbury.

Euphrasia is a former township in Grey County. Since 2001 it is a part of the municipality of Grey Highlands. Euphrasia is located east of Beaverdale, north of Wodehouse and southwest of Beaver Valley. Euphrasia has an elevation of 433 meters.

Markdale is a community in Grey County. Markdale was first settled in 1846. In 2001, Markdale was amalgamated with the townships of Artemesia, Euphrasia and Osprey to form Grey Highlands. On August 20, 2009, an F2 tornado originating in Durham touched down in Markdale and caused some local damage.

Arkwright was an important community in the early days of Bruce County's history. First settled in the 1850s, it gained prominence as both a supply centre and busy stopping place along the stage route. At its height Arkwright boasted two hotels, two stores, a wagon shop, two blacksmiths and a physician. A sawmill was located close by. There was also a school and two Methodist churches that later merged. A post office operated from 1857 to 1915 in one of the general stores.

  Arkwright served as the seat of township government for many years. The Township Council met regularly in the township hall. Lack of a railway prevented Arkwright from attracting any major industries.

  Tara is located in the municipality of Arran-Elderslie in Bruce County and is located on the Sauble River. Tara was named after a town in County Meath, Ireland which served as the seat of Irish royalty. Soon after the survey of the township was completed in 1851, John Hamilton and Richard Berford, early settlers in the area, located here along the river. The opening of the Owen Sound Post road stimulated the growth of a small community. Situated in a rich agricultural region with abundant water power, the settlement developed quickly. By 1861 Tara had saw and grist mills, a foundry producing agricultural implements, wagon works and a tannery. Hamilton opened a hotel to serve the incoming settlers of the surrounding townships. A post-office opened in 1862. In 1880, the local newspaper, *The Tara Leader* was first published. Tara became a thriving commercial and manufacturing centre and, in anticipation of the arrival of the Stratford and Huron Railway, it was incorporated as a village on January 1, 1881.

  One historic plaque tells about an athlete, "Cyclone" Taylor 1885 – 1979, an outstanding hockey player who was born in Tara and began his amateur career with the Listowel Juniors about 1901. His exceptional skating ability and irrepressible energy drew widespread attention to Taylor and in 1905 in Michigan he entered the International League, hockey's first professional organization. Having joined the Canadian civil service in 1907, he continued to play with

Ottawa and Renfrew teams, and soon confirmed his reputation as a brilliant all-round player. He concluded his celebrated hockey career with the Vancouver Millionaires, 1912-20, of the Pacific Coast Hockey Association. In 1946 he received the Order of the British Empire for his service to the immigration department. "Cyclone" Taylor was elected to the Hockey Hall of Fame in 1947.

The second plaque refers to a prominent lawyer. "Sir William H. Hearst 1864 - 1941. Born in Arran Township, Hearst was educated at the Collingwood Collegiate and Osgoode Hall. He practised law at Sault Ste. Marie and was first elected to the provincial legislature as Conservative member for that community in 1908. He was appointed minister of lands, forests and mines in 1911 during the administration of Sir James Whitney, and following the latter's death in September, 1914, became Ontario's seventh prime minister. Hearst retained that post throughout the First World War and was knighted for his services. Following his government's defeat in 1919 by the United Farmers of Ontario, he retired from politics, but served as a member of the International Joint Commission on Boundary Waters, 1920-40.

Williscroft was a farming hamlet, located in Bruce County, first settled around 1850. By 1856 it had a post office, followed by a school in 1858. The village quickly grew to include a blacksmith shop, a store, two coopers, a door and sash building business, and saw and grist mills. A Baptist church was added in 1875. Later industries in Williscroft included a cheese factory and woodworking and carriage shops. Farm based organizations, which took hold during the 1880s, led to the construction of a large Grange Hall, also used as a community and social centre, and later as an Orange Lodge.

Chatsworth

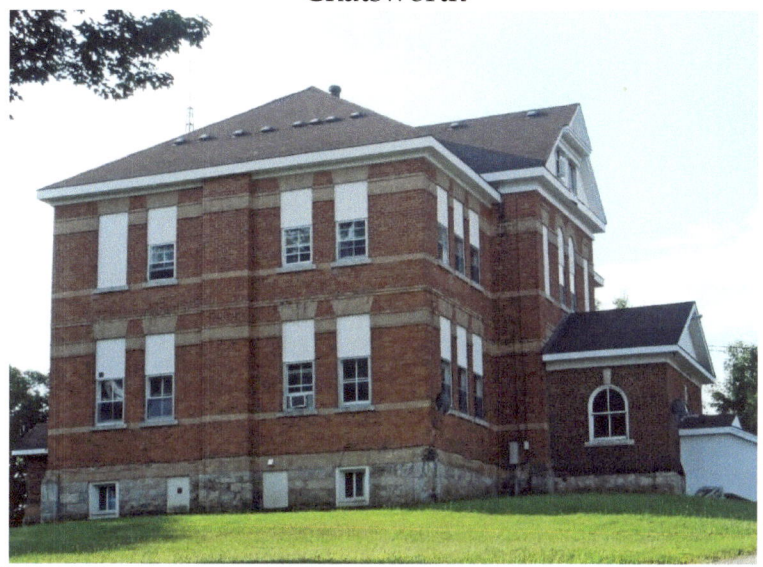

777346 Ontario 10 - Holland-Chatsworth Central School – banding, voussoirs

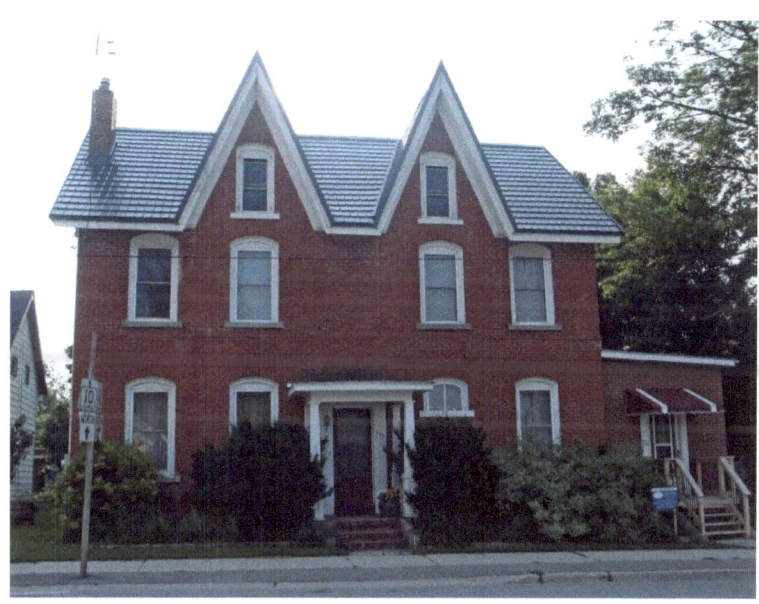

#141 - Gothic

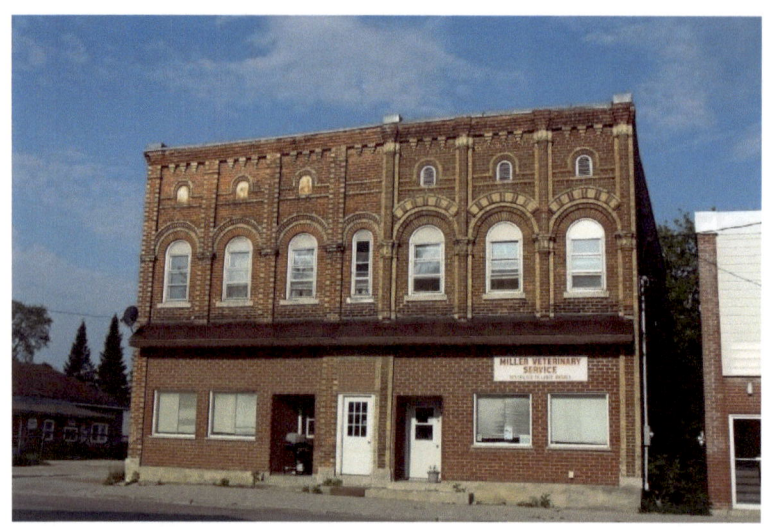

271 Garafraxa Street – Miller Veterinary Service – pilasters, dichromatic brickwork, voussoirs

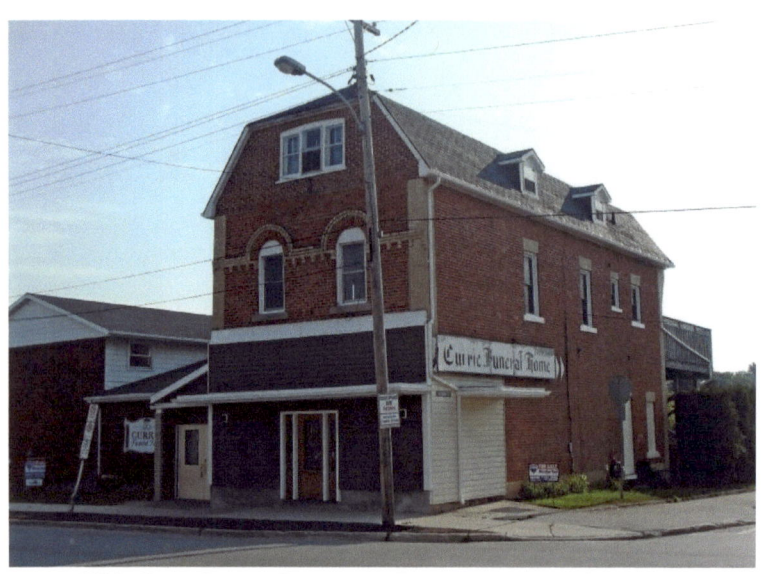

251 Garafraxa Street – Currie Funeral Home

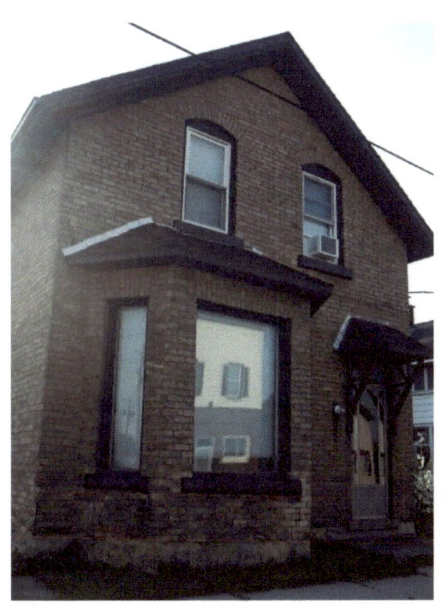

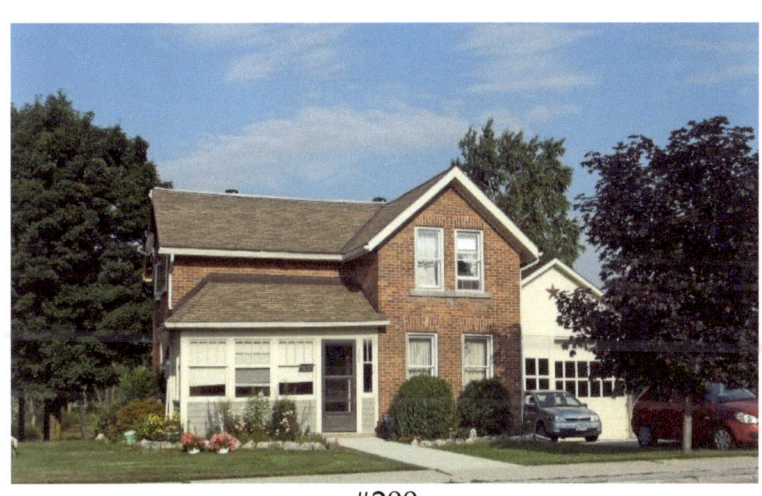

#200

Chatsworth

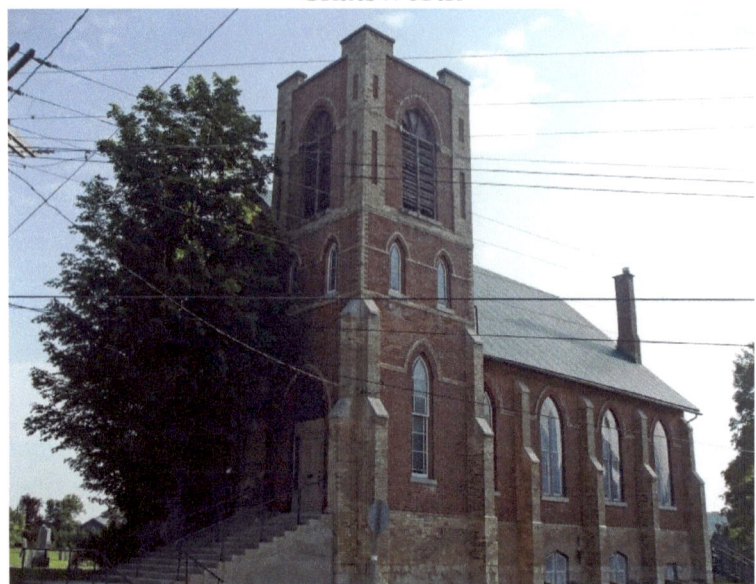

43 Toronto Street - Chatsworth United Church – lancet windows, buttresses, three-storey tower

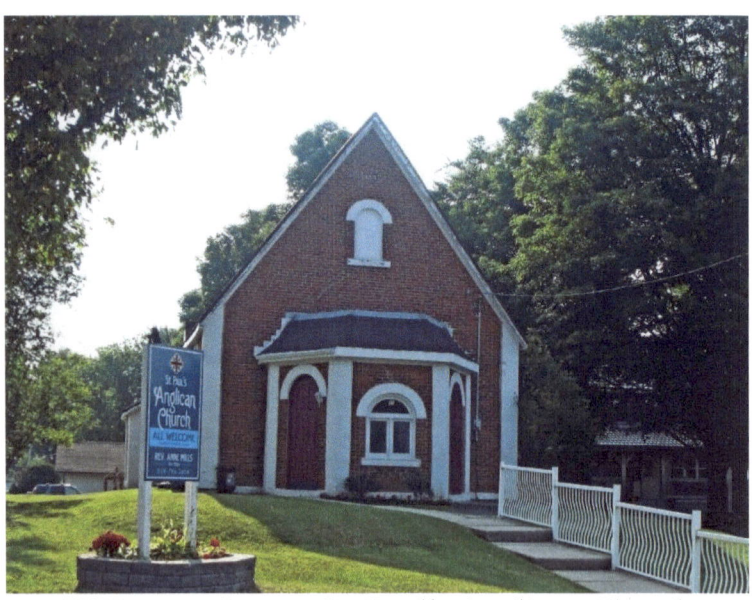

57 Toronto Street - St. Paul's Anglican Church

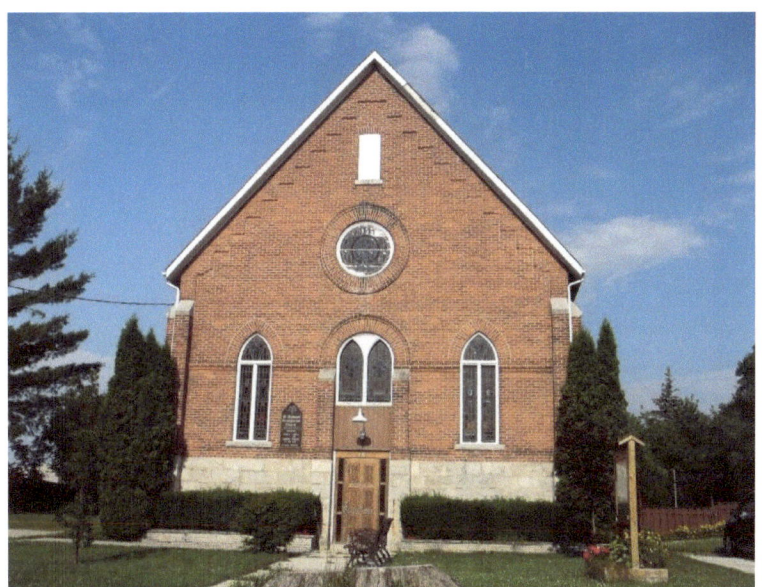

22 John Street - St. Andrew's Presbyterian Church – lancet windows, rose window

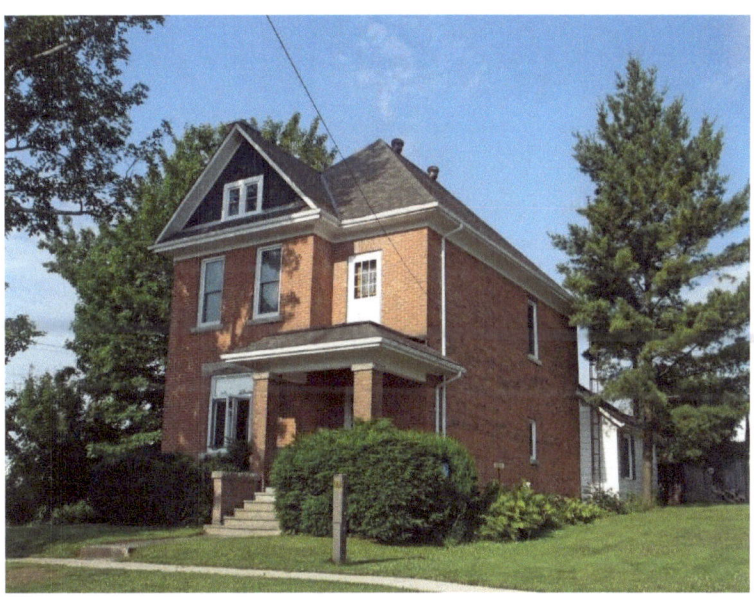

Edwardian

Chatsworth

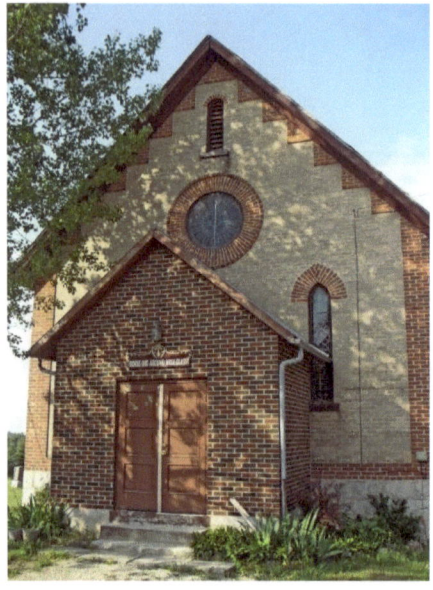

#776186 - Stained Glass Studio – rose window, lancet windows

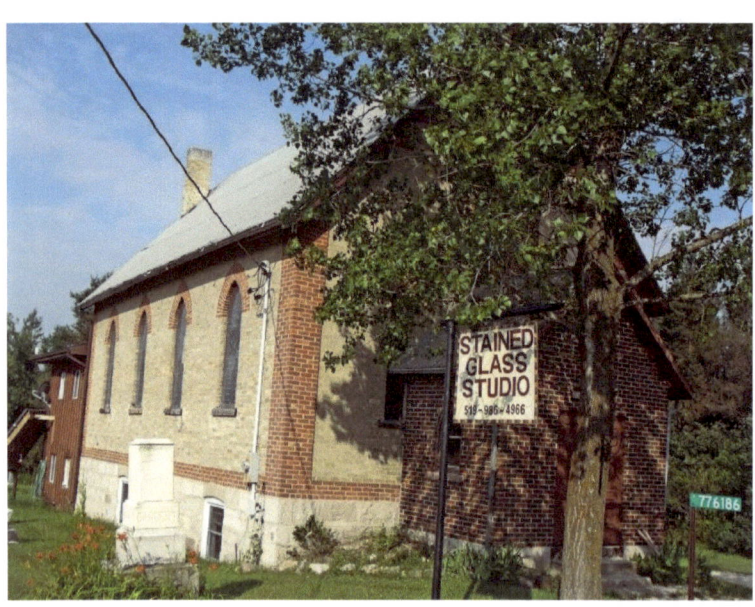

Desboro

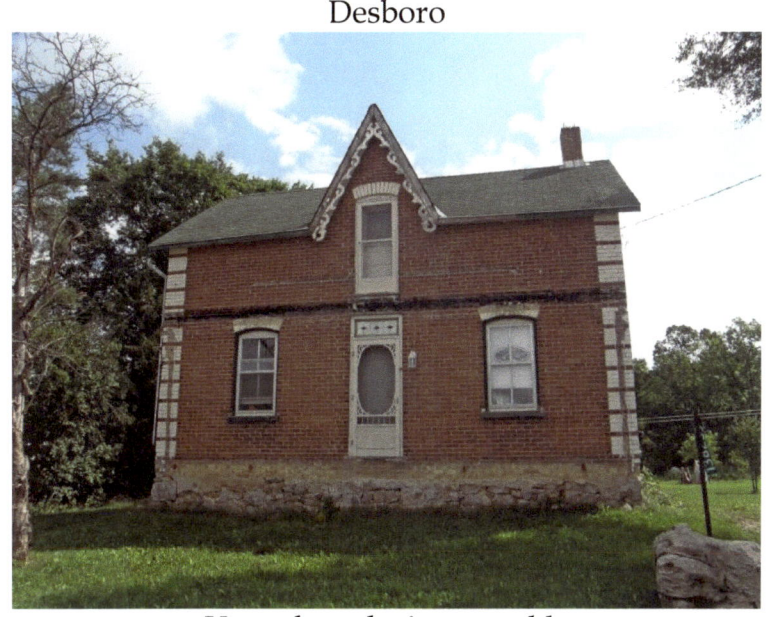

Verge board trim on gable

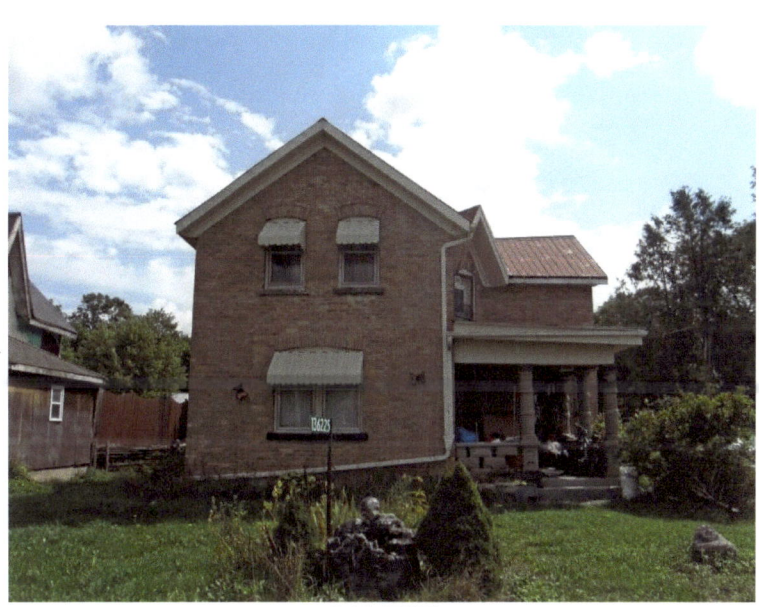

#136225

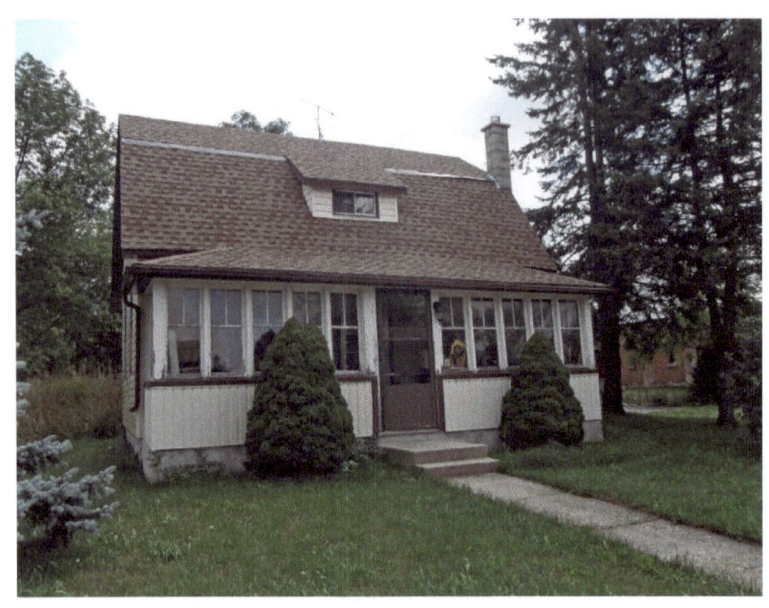

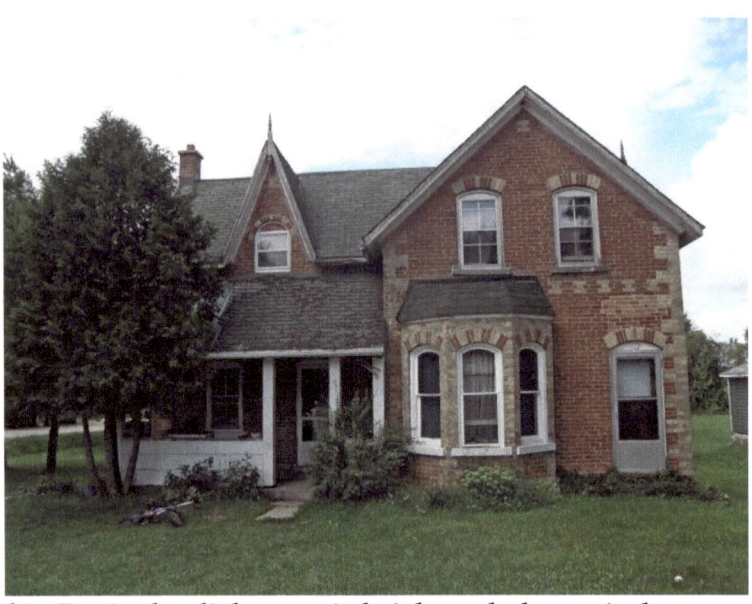

Gothic Revival – dichromatic brickwork, bay window, corner quoins

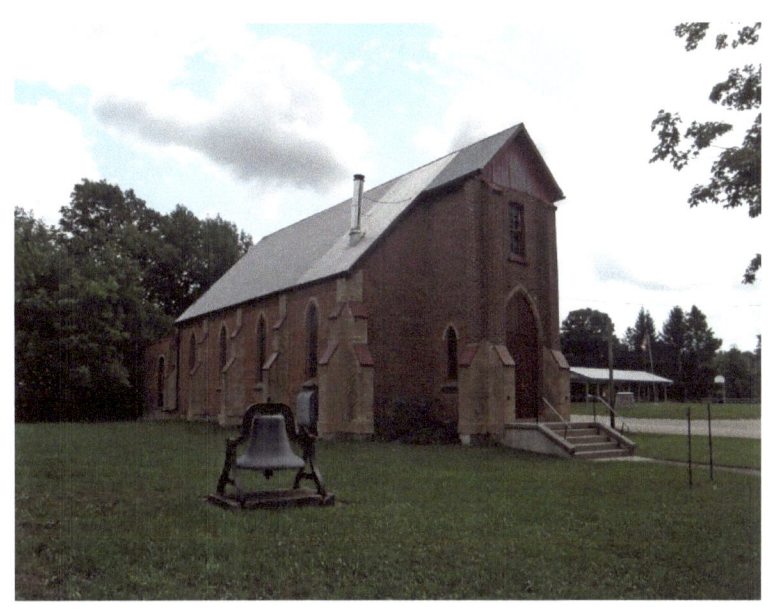

Buttresses, lancet windows

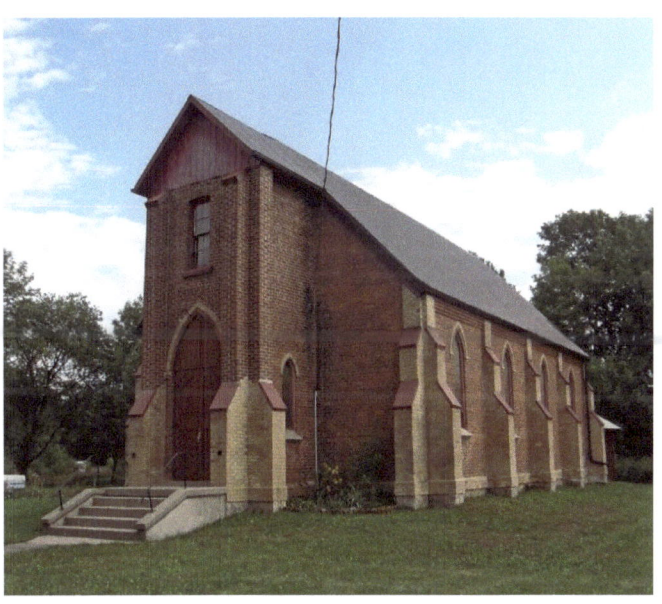

Desboro

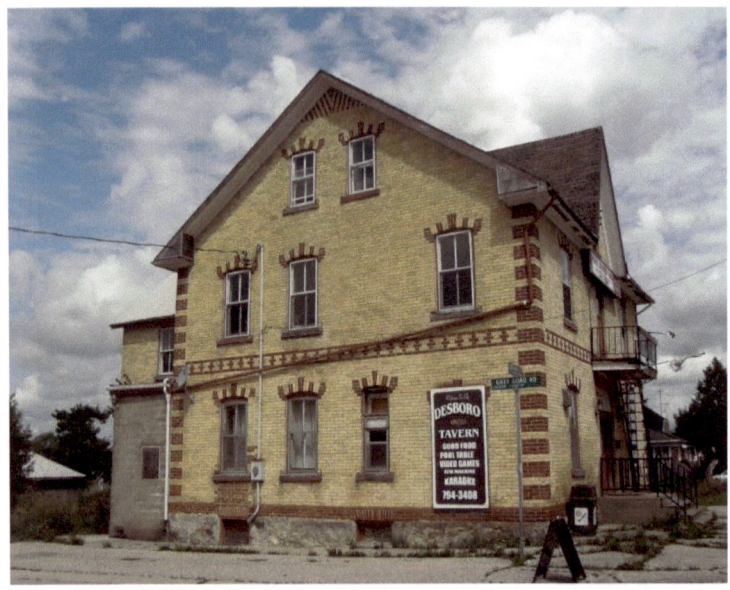

481 Grey Road 40 - Desboro Tavern – dichromatic brickwork, banding, corner quoins

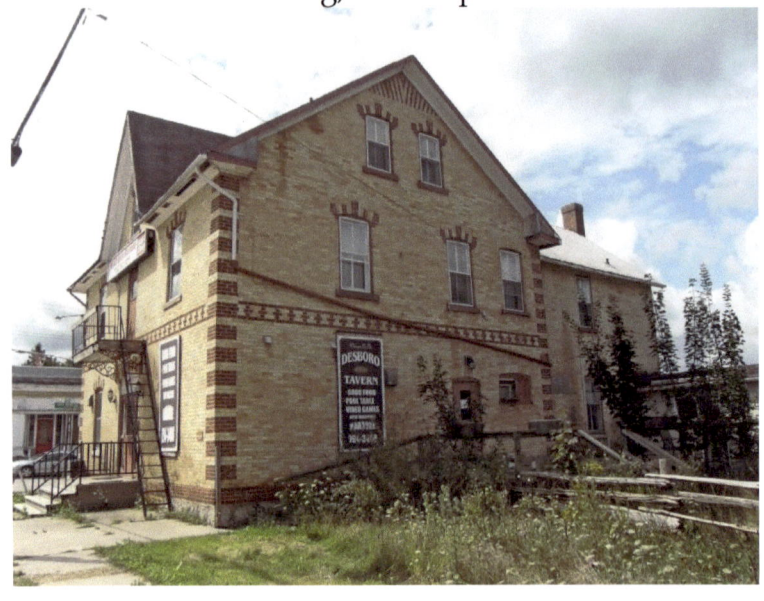

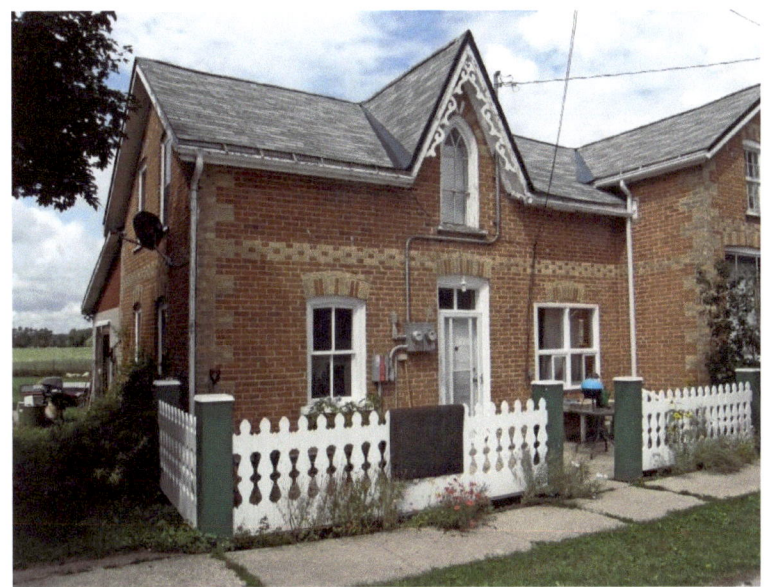

Gothic – dichromatic banding, corner quoins, verge board trim on gable

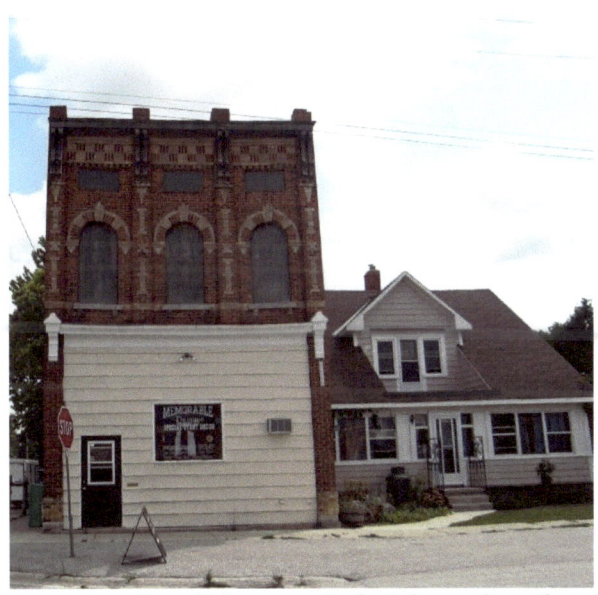

Concession 8 – dichromatic brickwork, pilasters

Desboro

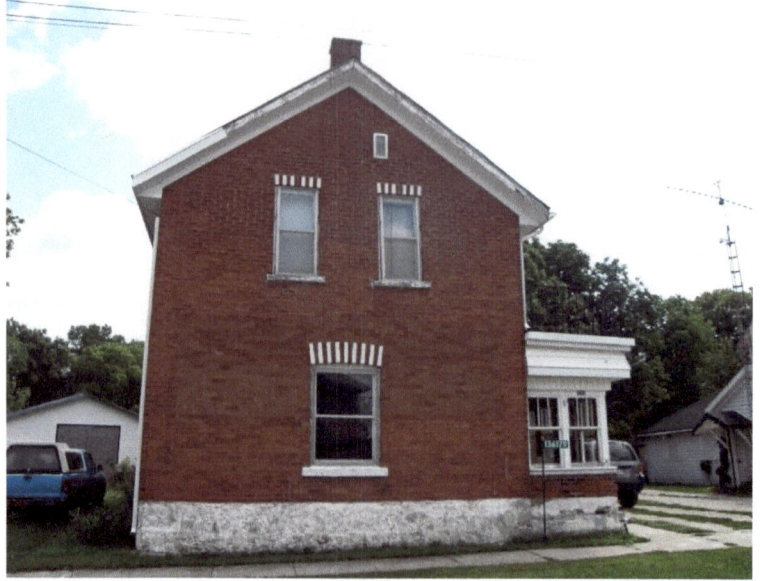

#136179

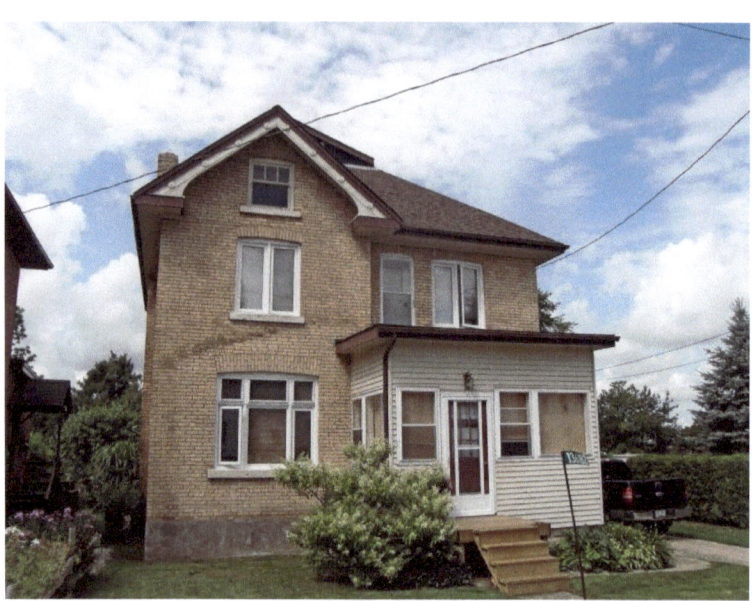

#136182

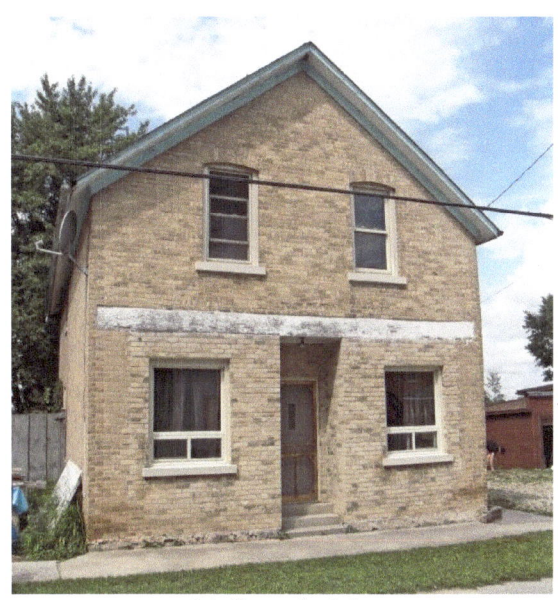

Yellow brick

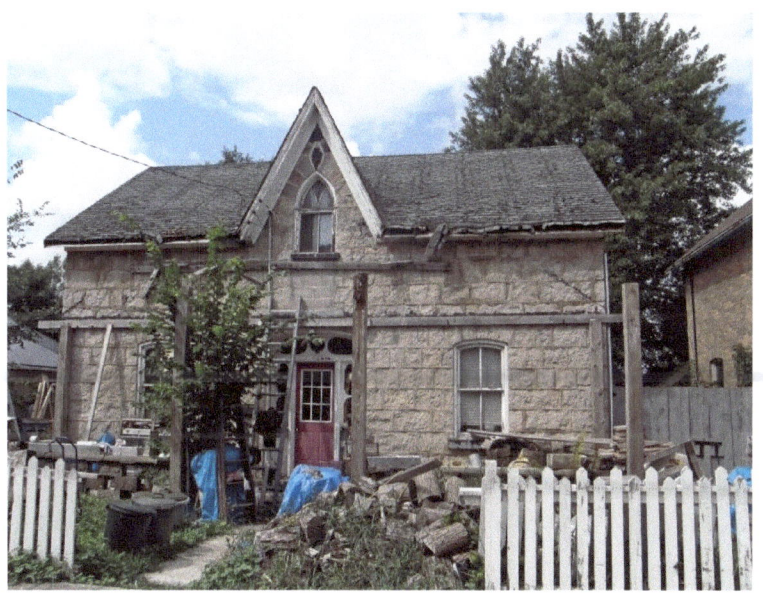

Gothic Regency Cottage

Desboro

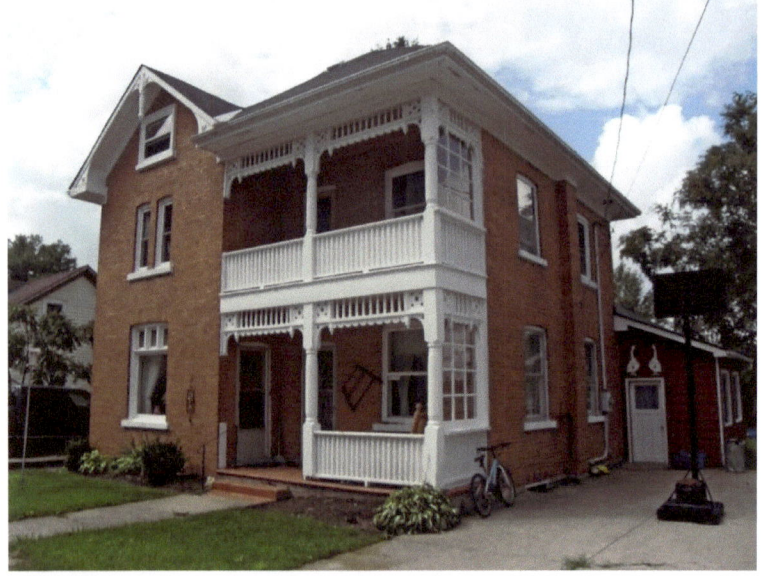

Italianate – two-storey verandas with spindle work

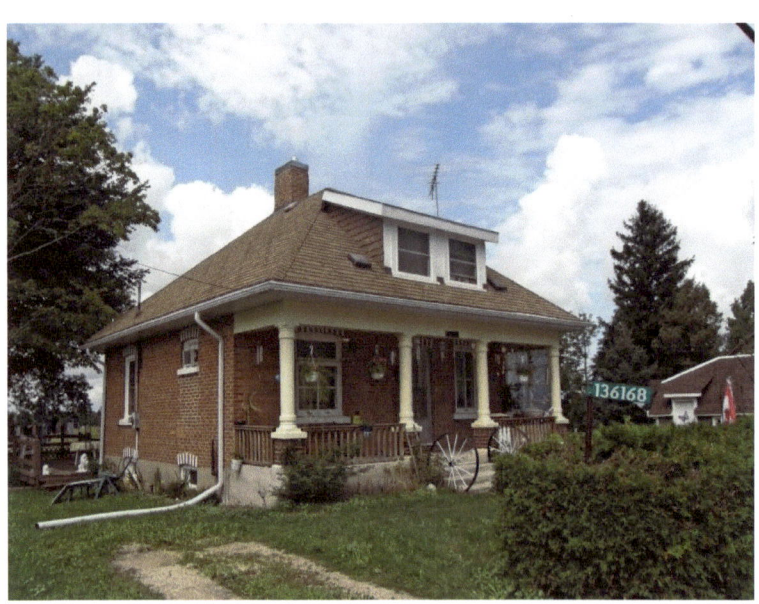

#136168 – dormer in the hipped roof

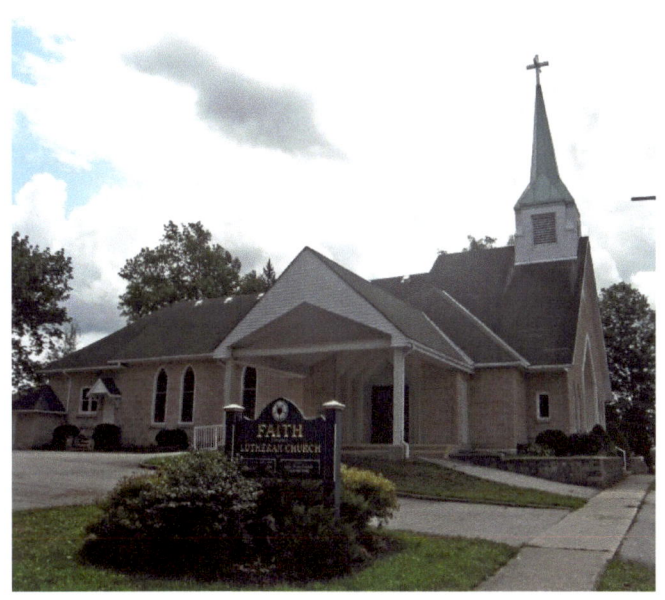

136167 Concession Road 8 - Faith Lutheran Church

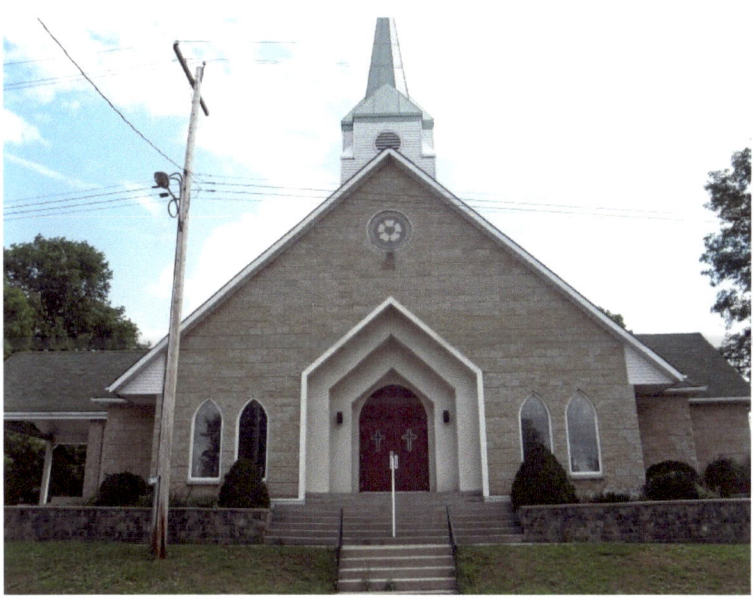

Desboro

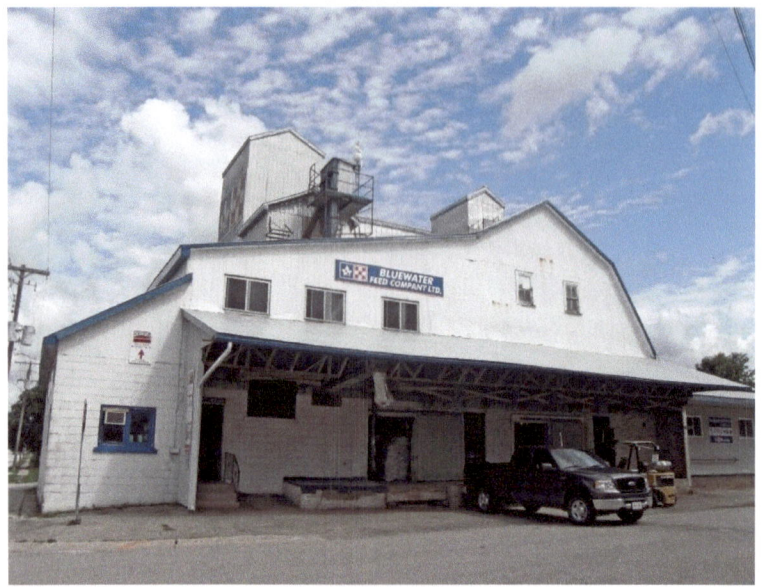

Bluewater Feed Company Limited

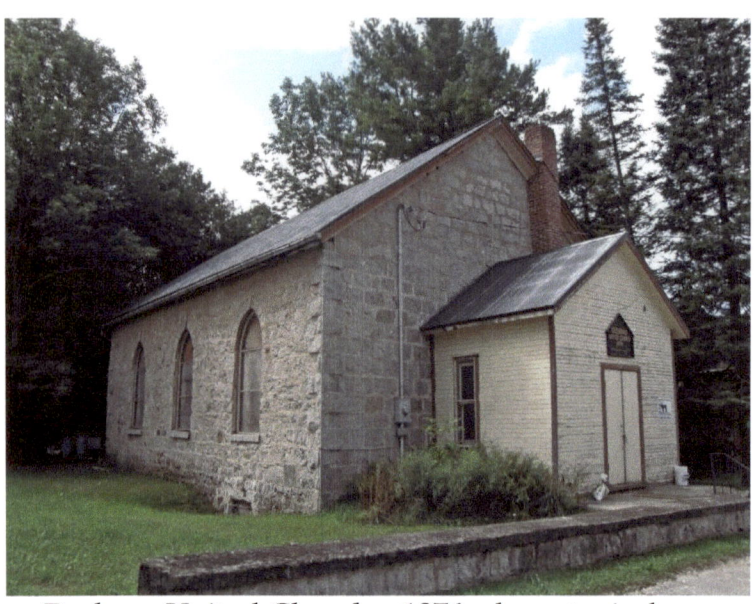

Desboro United Church – 1876 – lancet windows

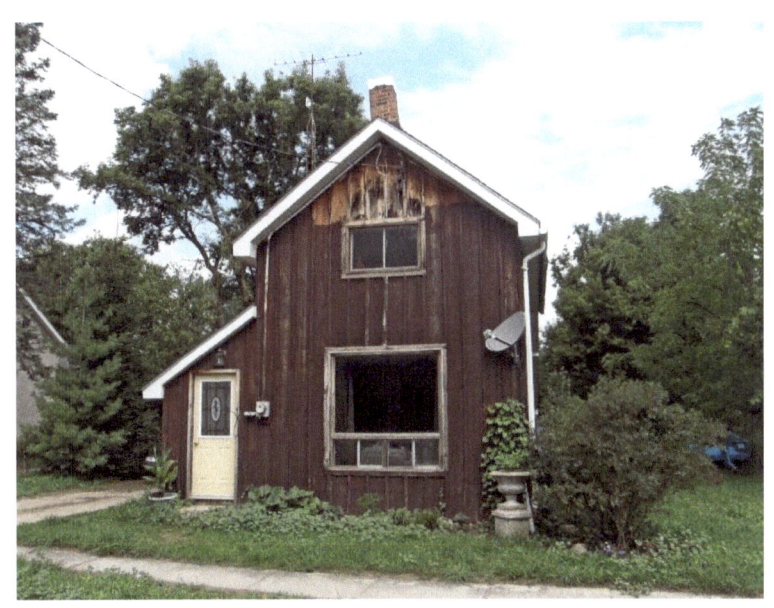

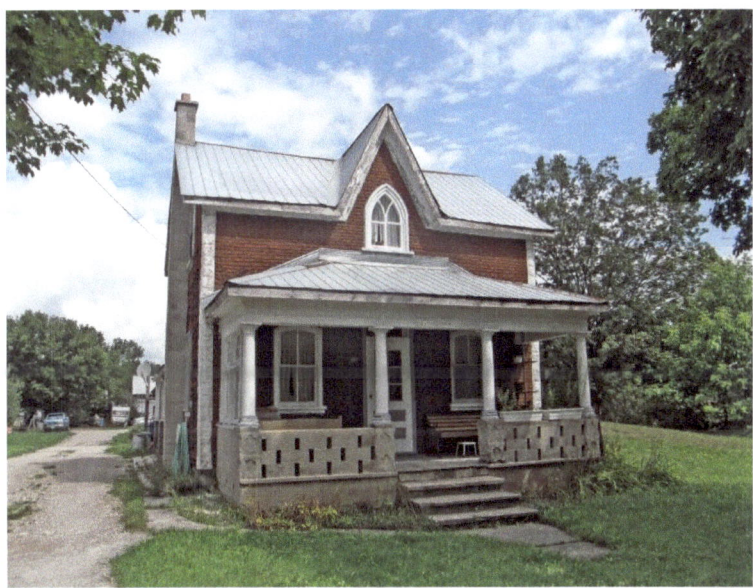

Gothic

Desboro

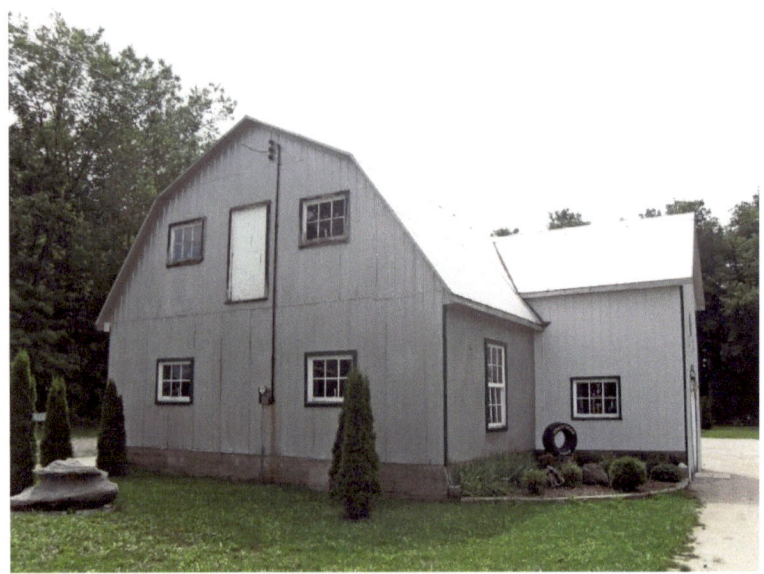

Gambrel roof

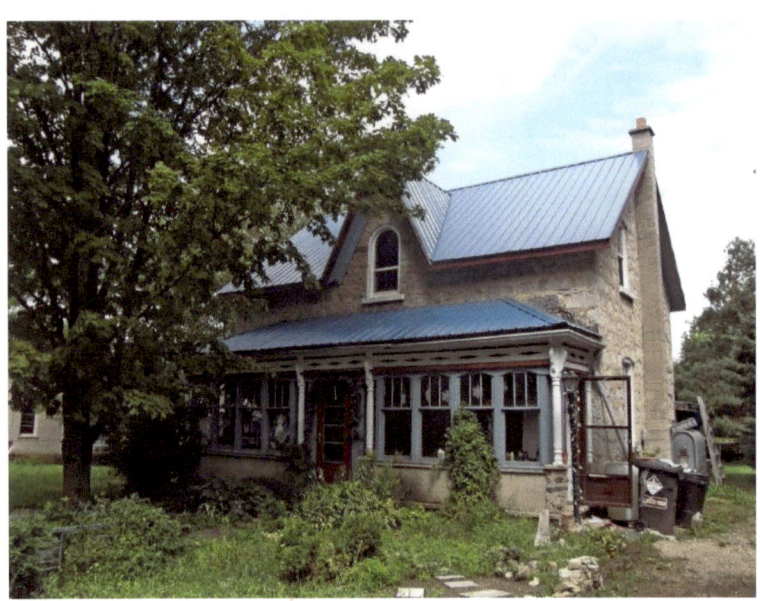

Gothic

Dornoch

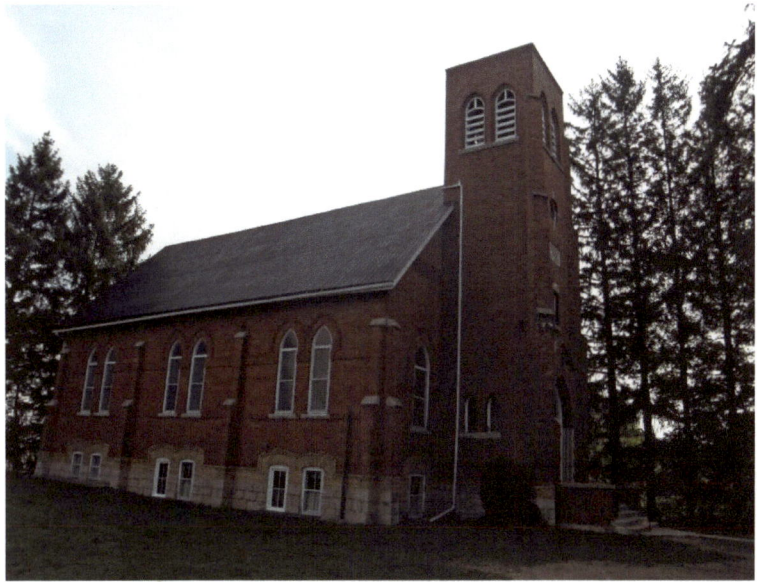

Latona Presbyterian Church, Dornoch – 1920 – lancet windows, three-storey rectangular tower

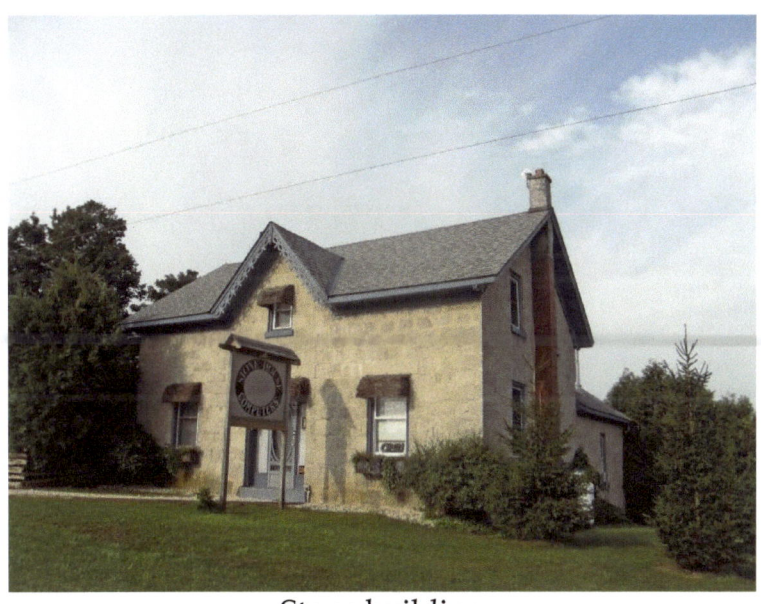

Stone building

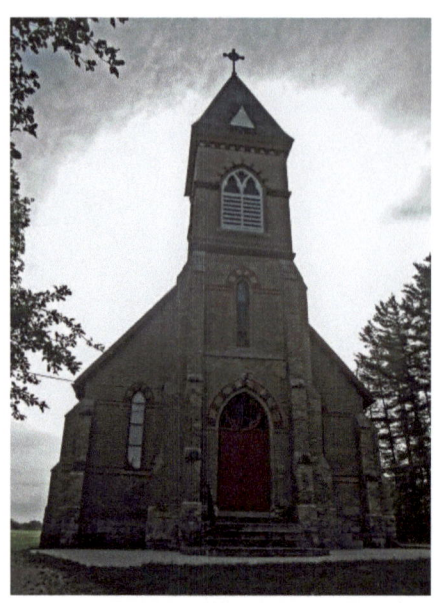

St. Paul's Catholic Church, Dornoch

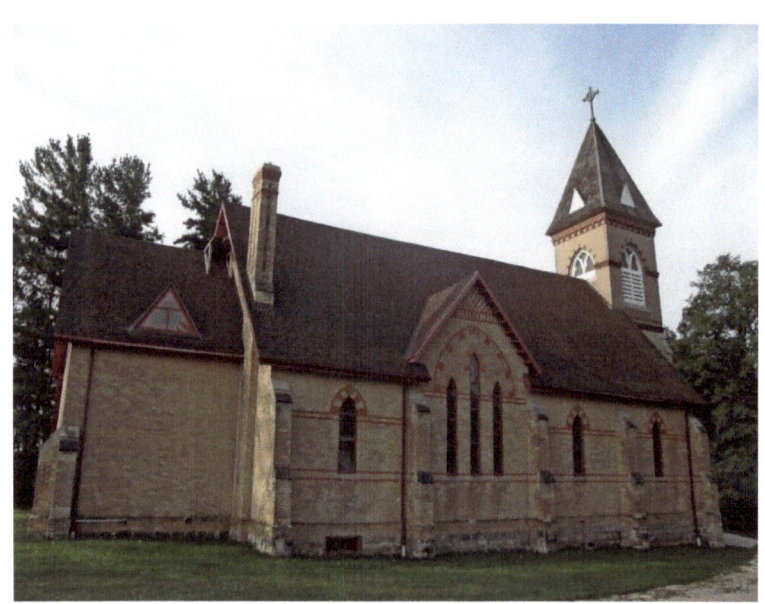

Gothic – lancet windows, banding, dichromatic brickwork, three-storey tower

Grey Road 40 and Grey Road 3

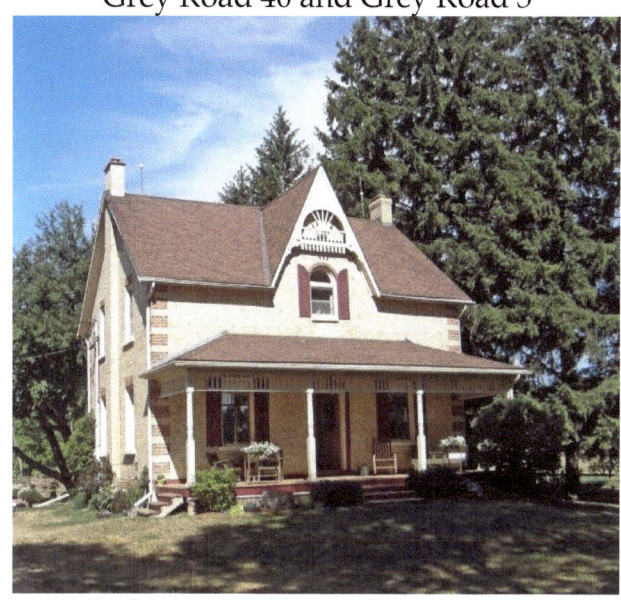

Gothic – spindle work in the gable

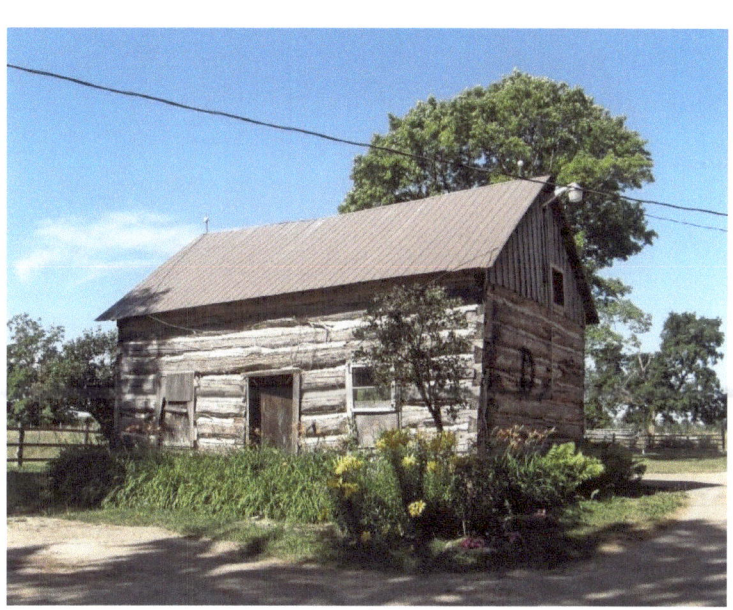

Log barn

Grey Road 40 and Grey Road 3

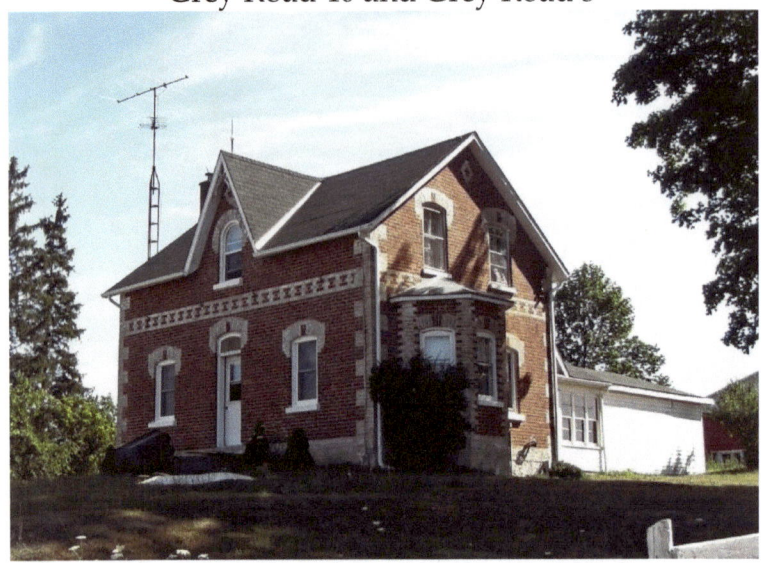

Gothic, red brick, dichromatic brickwork, banding, quoins, bay window, voussoirs and keystones

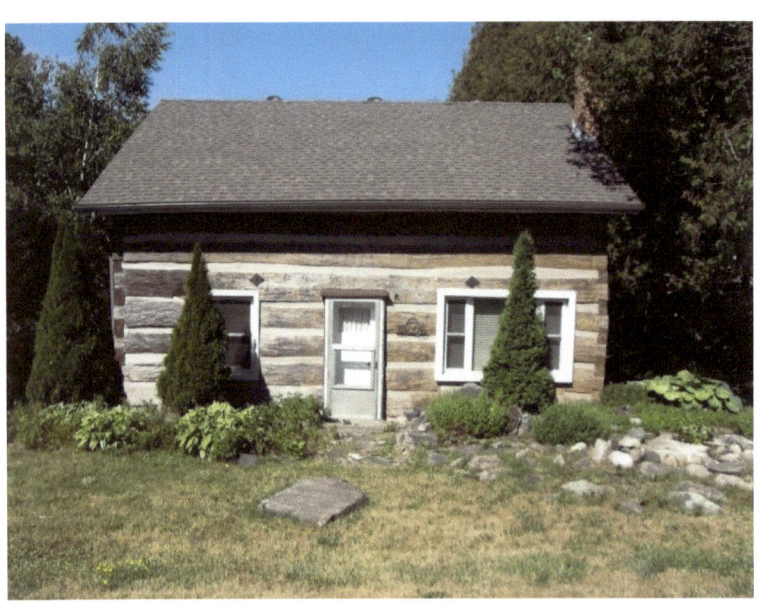

Log cabin

Williamsford

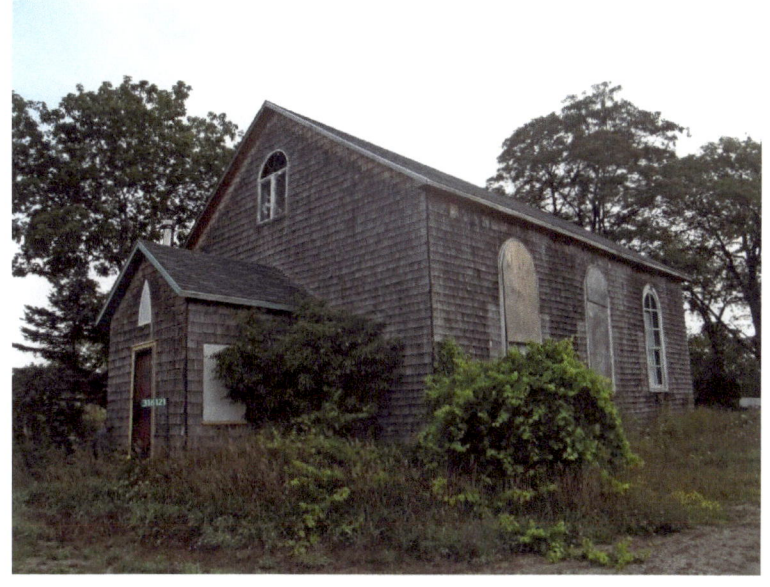

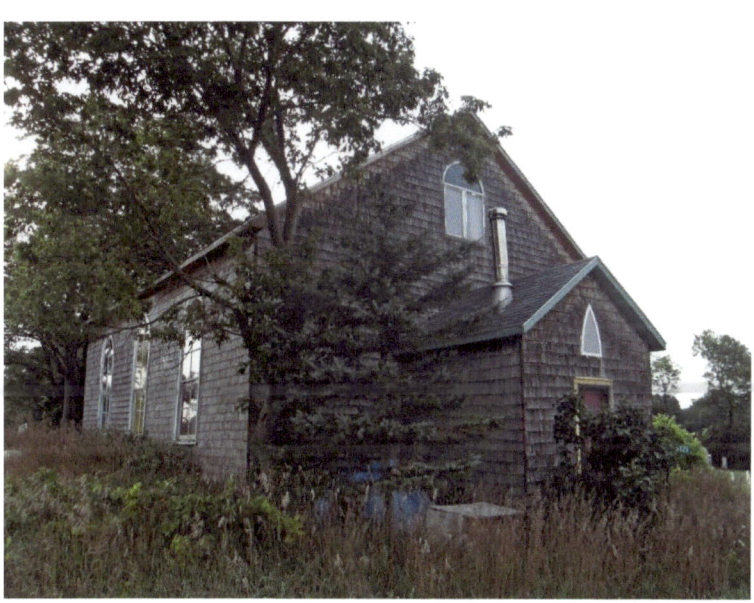

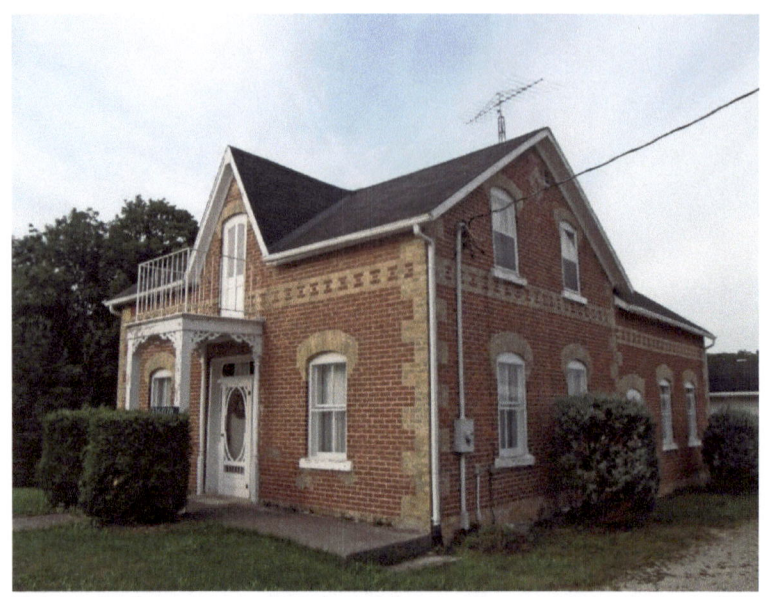

Gothic – dichromatic brickwork, corner quoins, second floor balcony, voussoirs

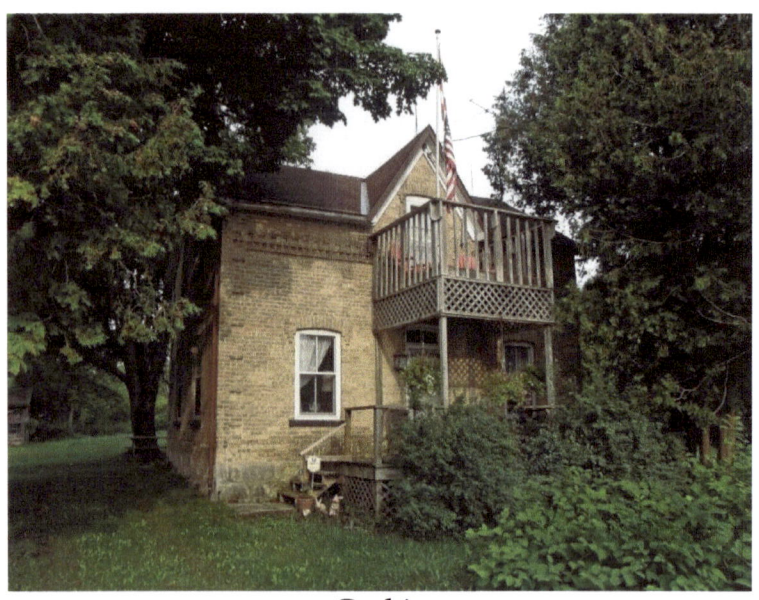

Gothic

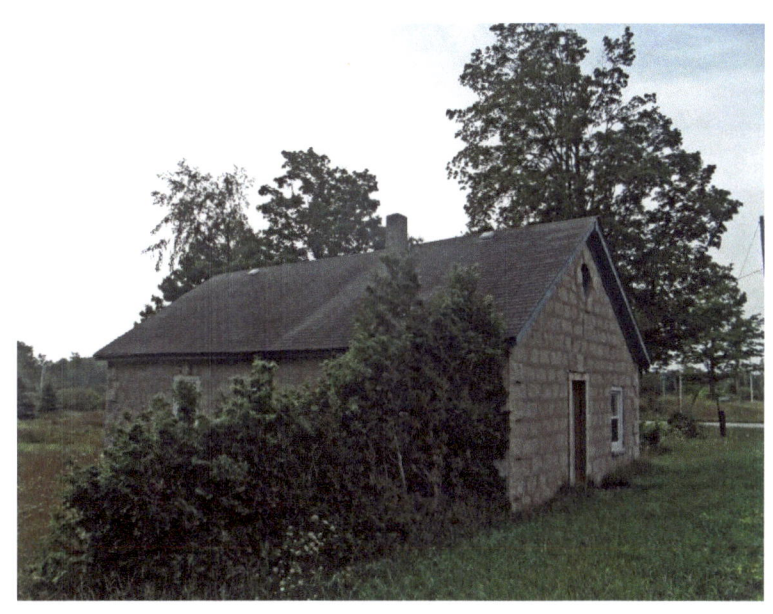

A.D. 1888 – stone

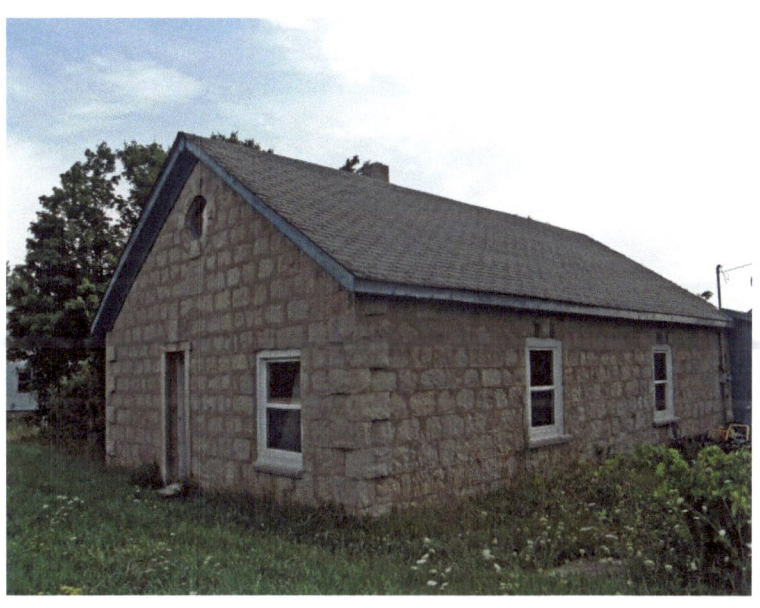

Marmion

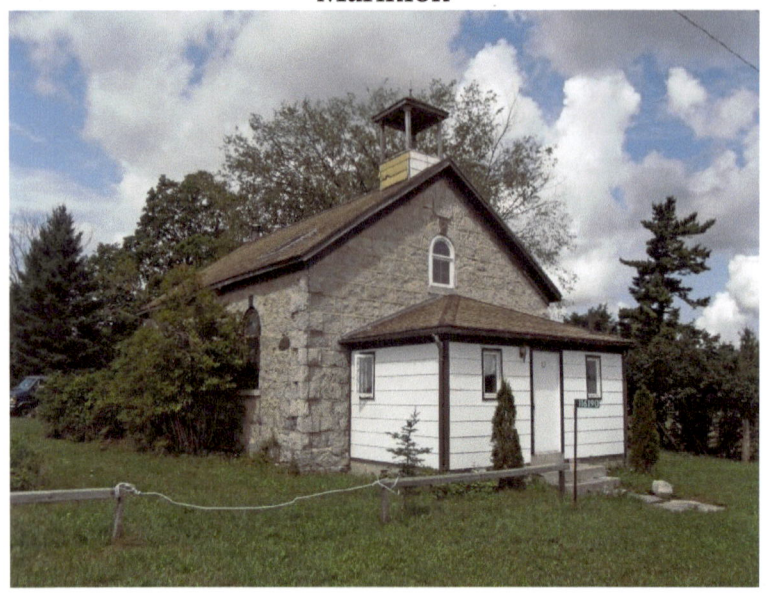

S.S. No. 6 School – 1877

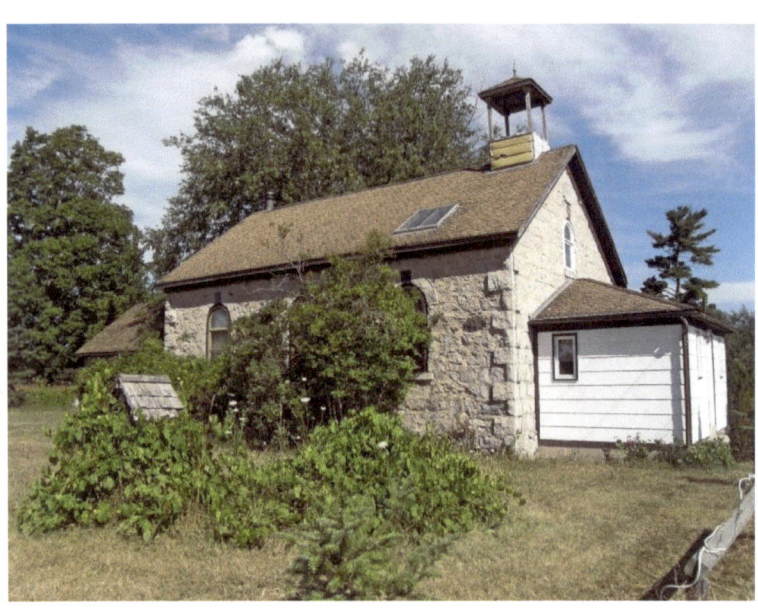

Keady

Chalmers United Church, Keady – battlement on top of three-storey tower

Elmwood

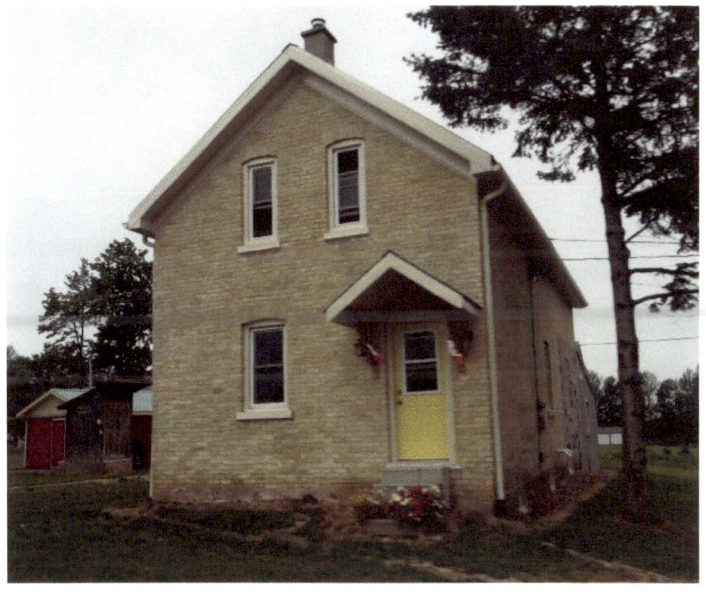

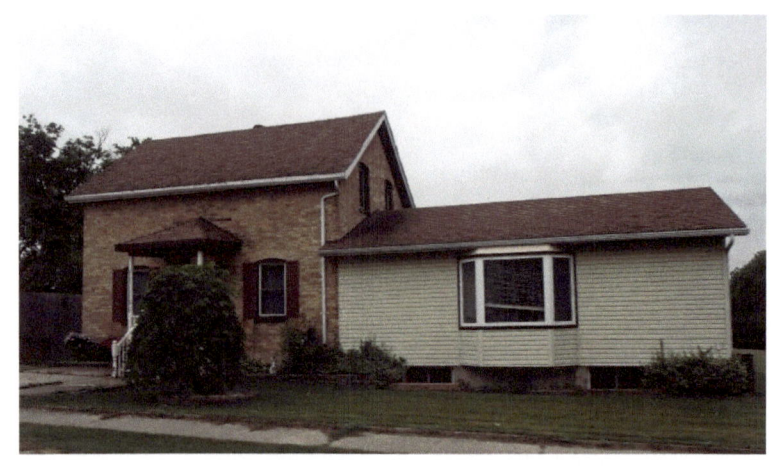

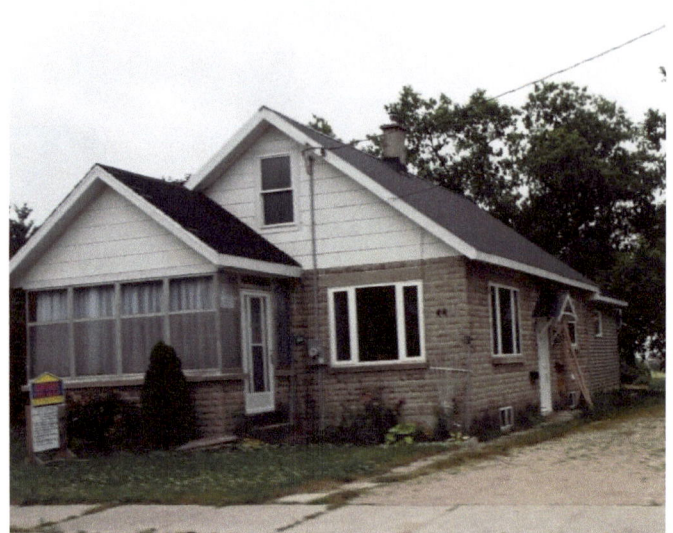

#44

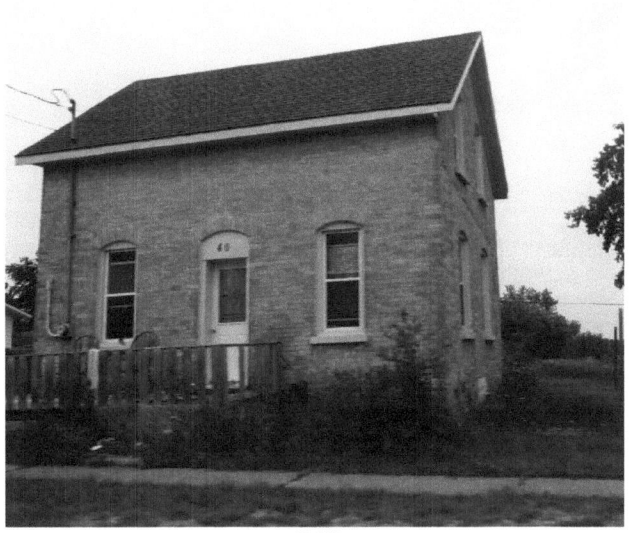

#40

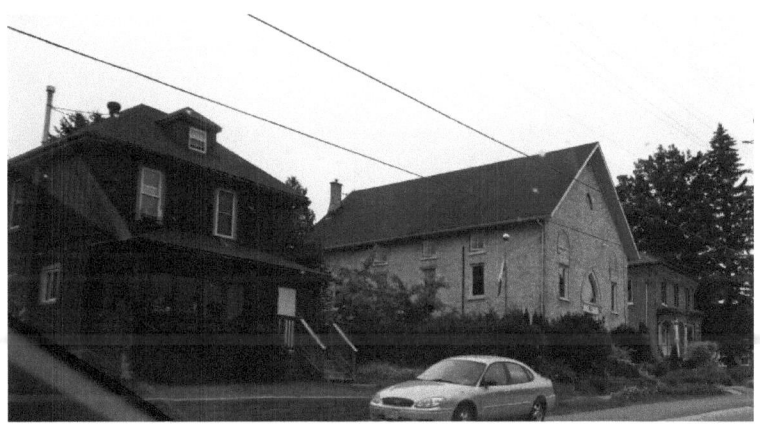

The yellow brick building is the former Elmwood church building. It is now an apartment building.

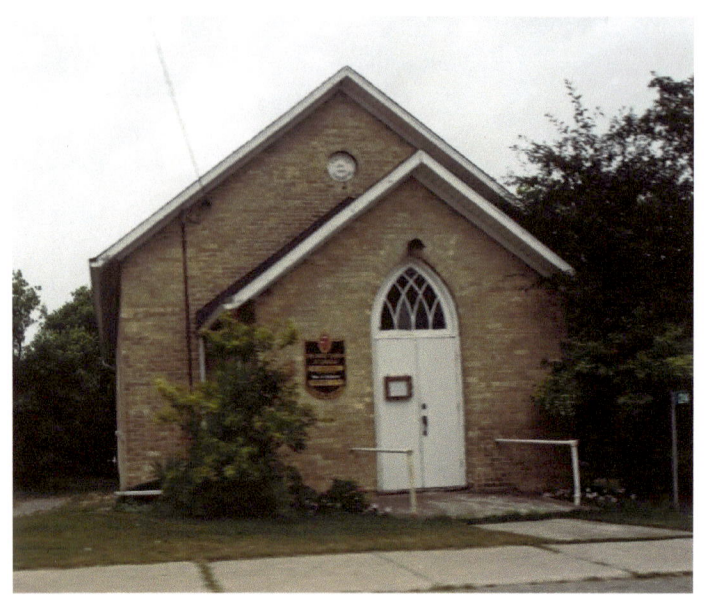

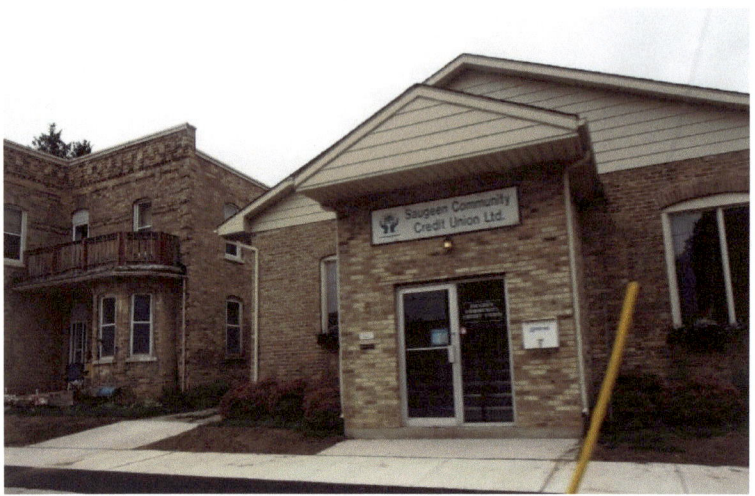

6 Main Street South - Saugeen Community Credit Union

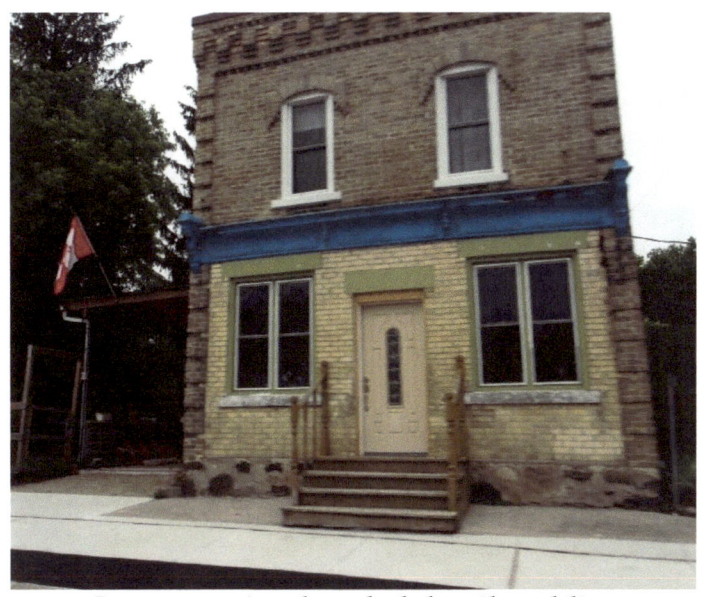

Corner quoins, beveled dentil molding

Duncan

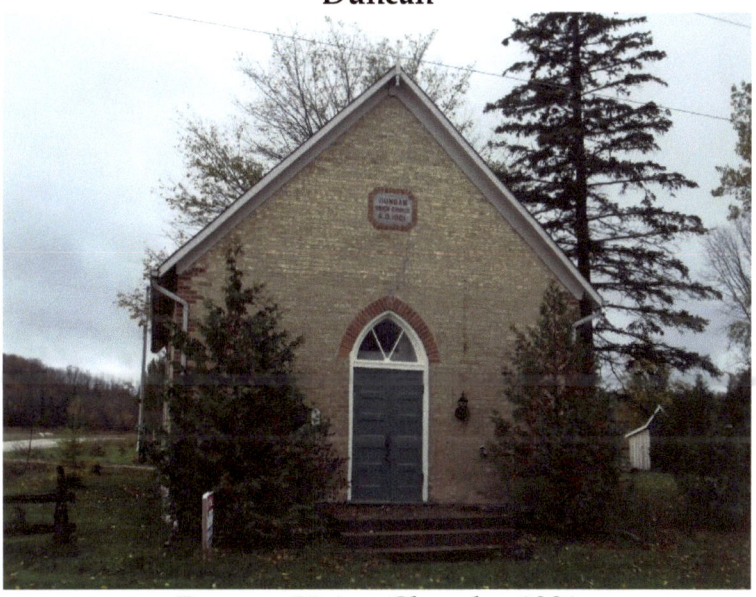

Duncan Union Church - 1901

Euphrasia

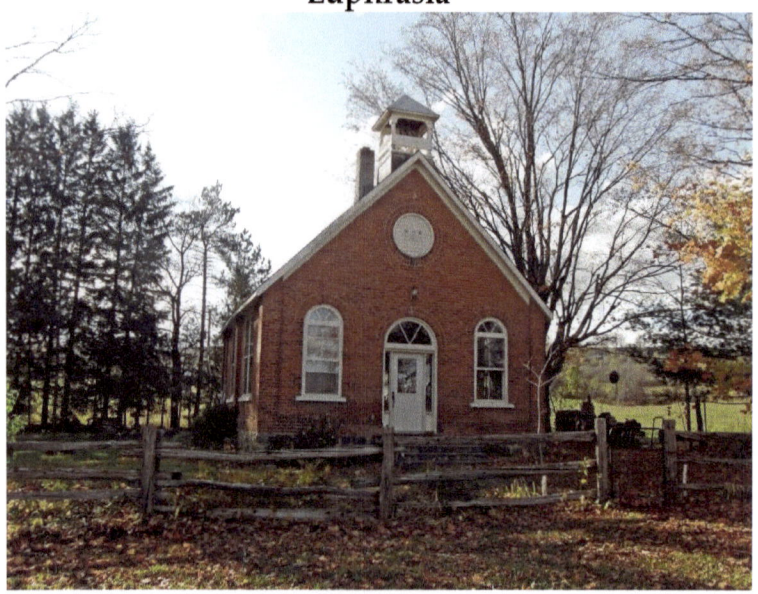

No. 21 Euphrasia – 1900

Markdale

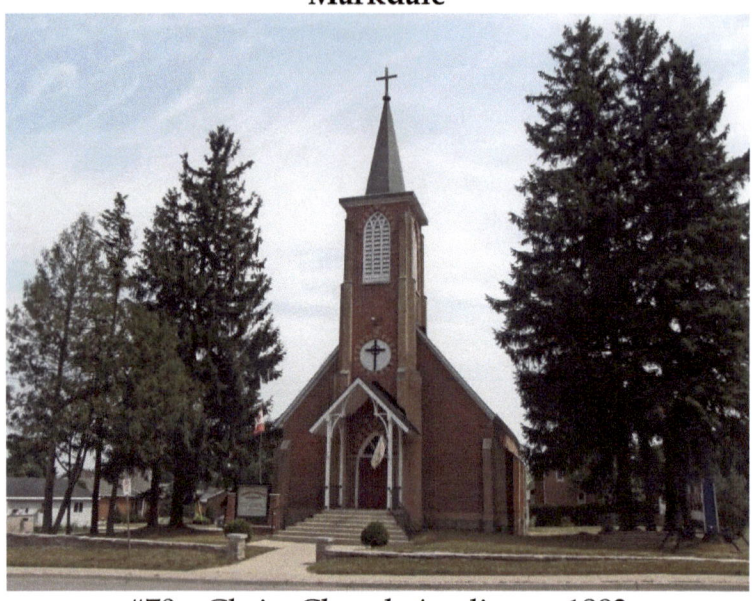

#70 – Christ Church Anglican – 1893

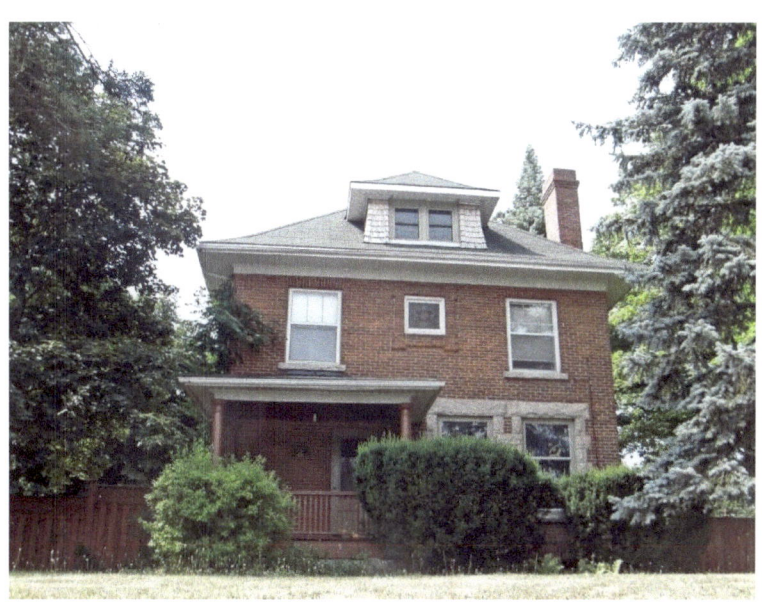

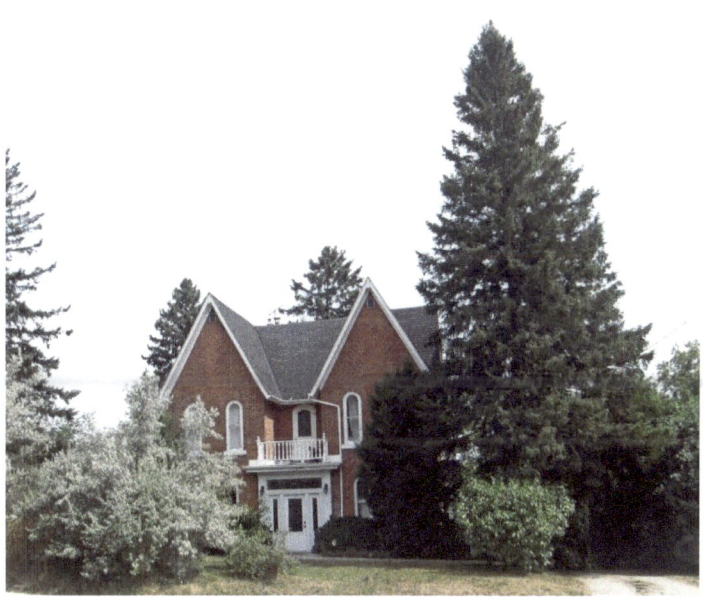

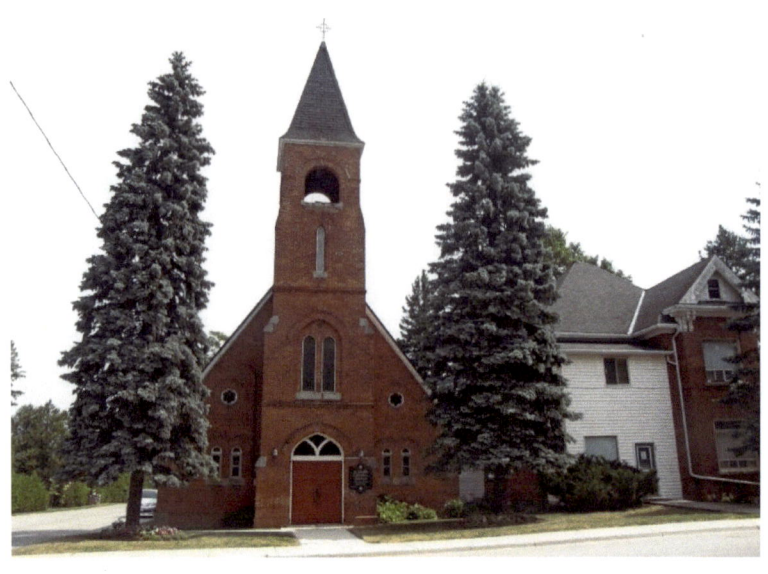

St. Joseph's Catholic Church – four-storey tower, buttresses

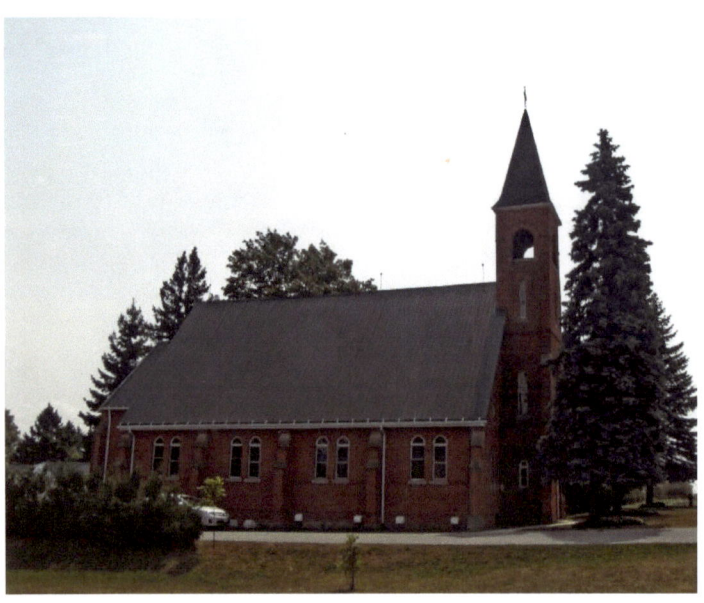

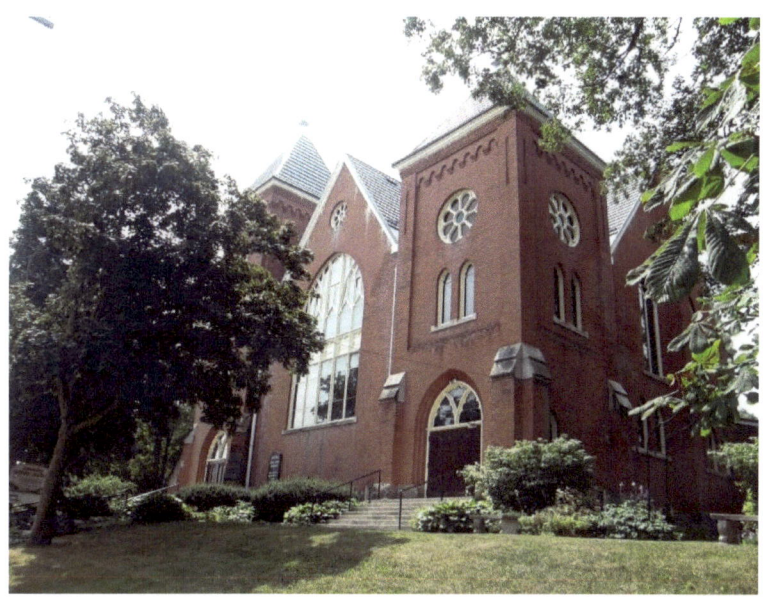

82 Toronto Street South - Annesley United Church, Markdale – 1906 – windows with muntins, rose window, three-storey tower with beveled dentil molding

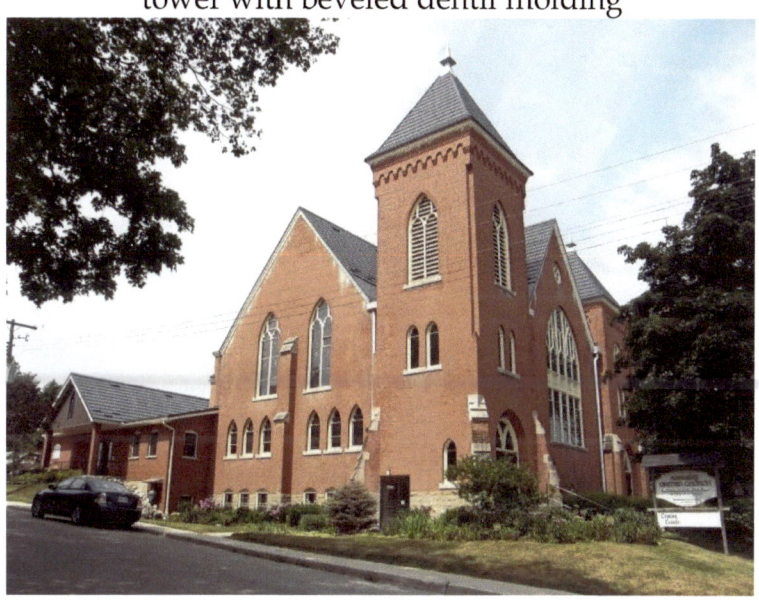

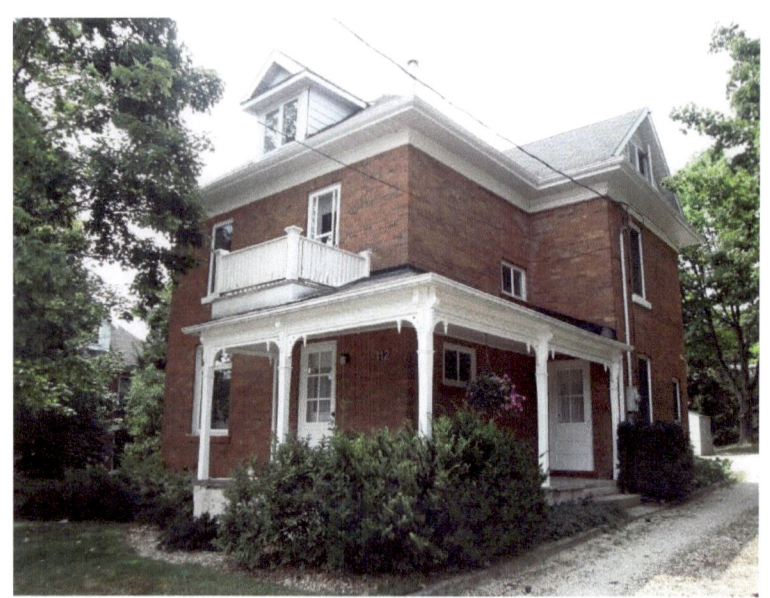
Dormer in roof, second floor balcony

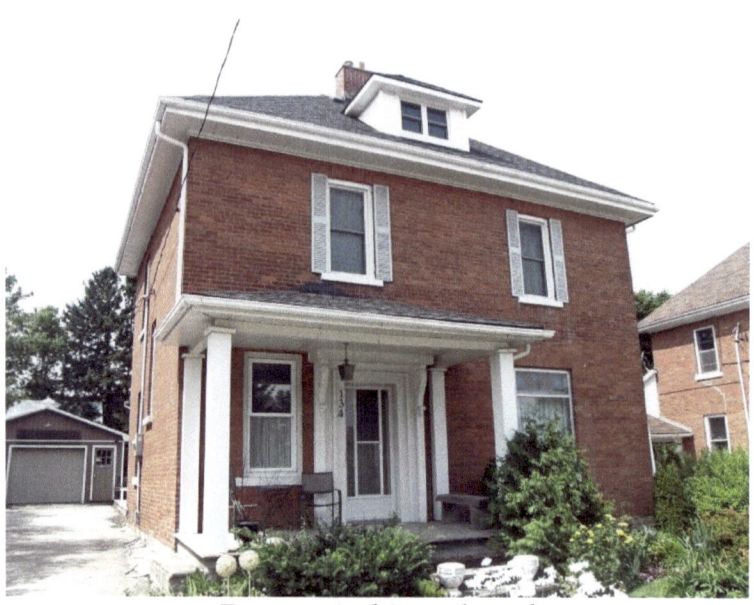
Dormer in hipped roof

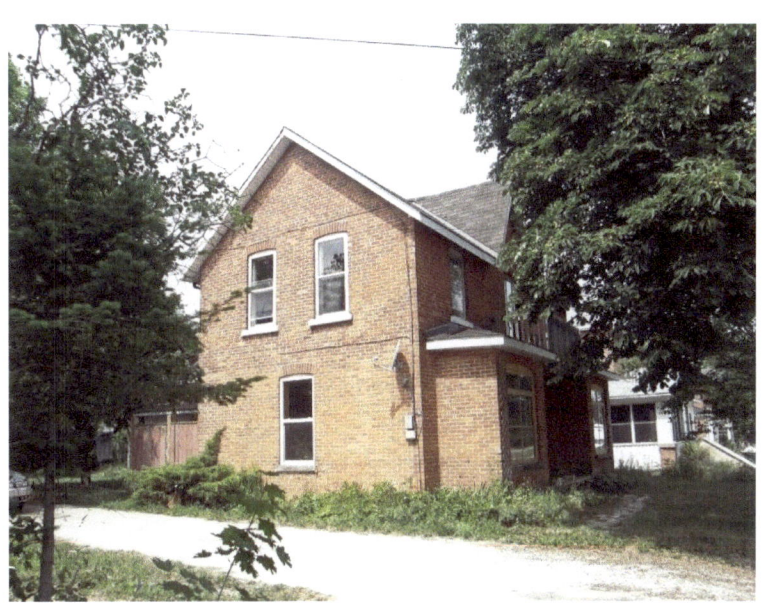
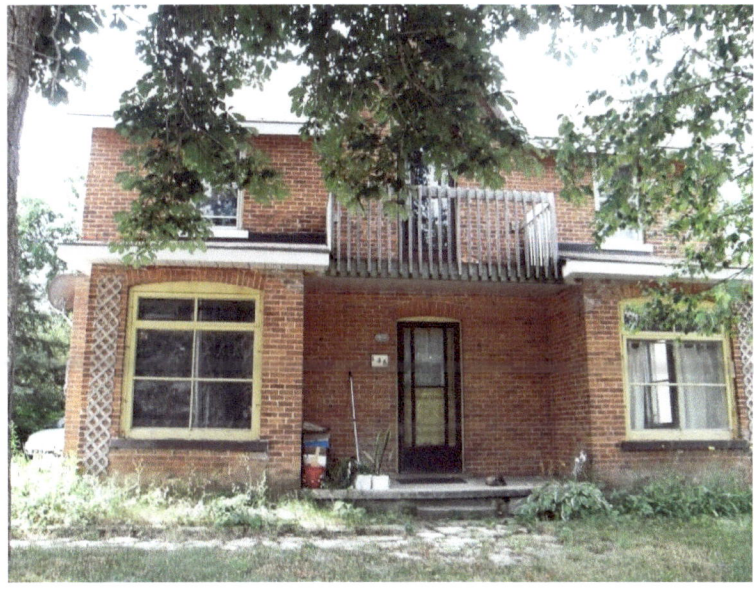

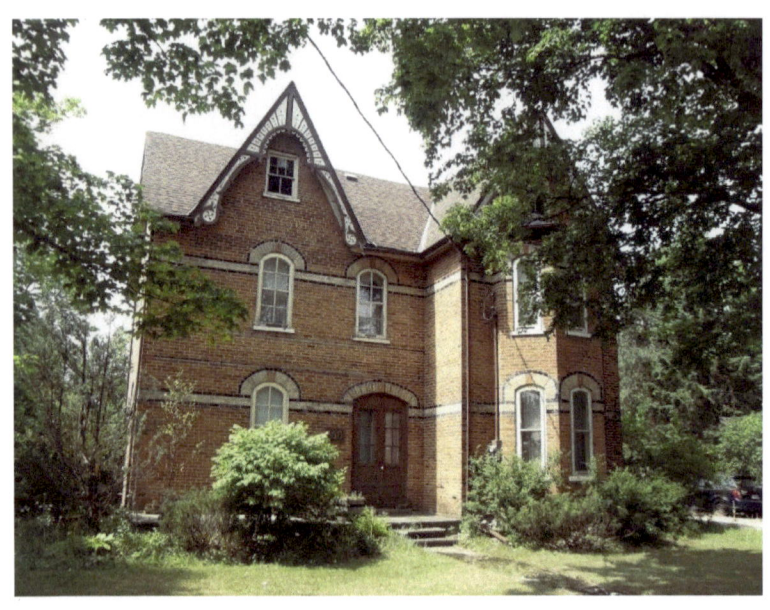

Verge board trim on gable, banding, voussoirs

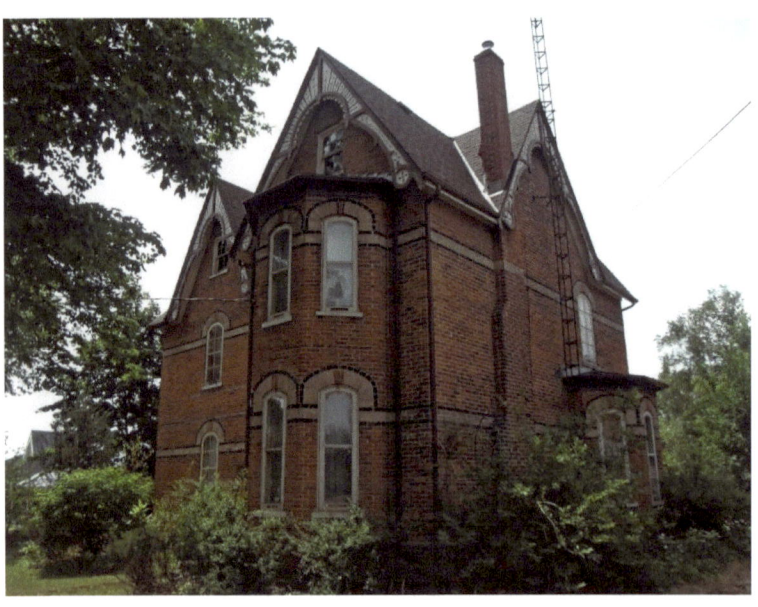

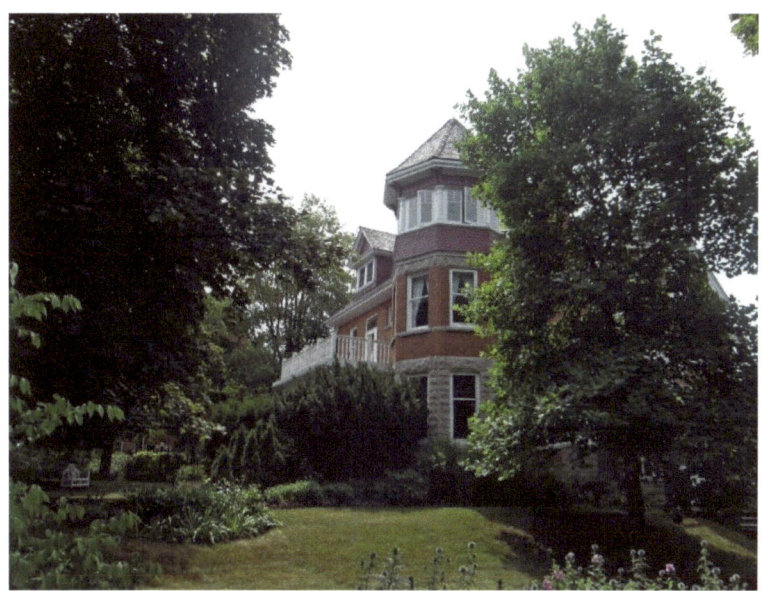

Three-storey turret

Arkwright

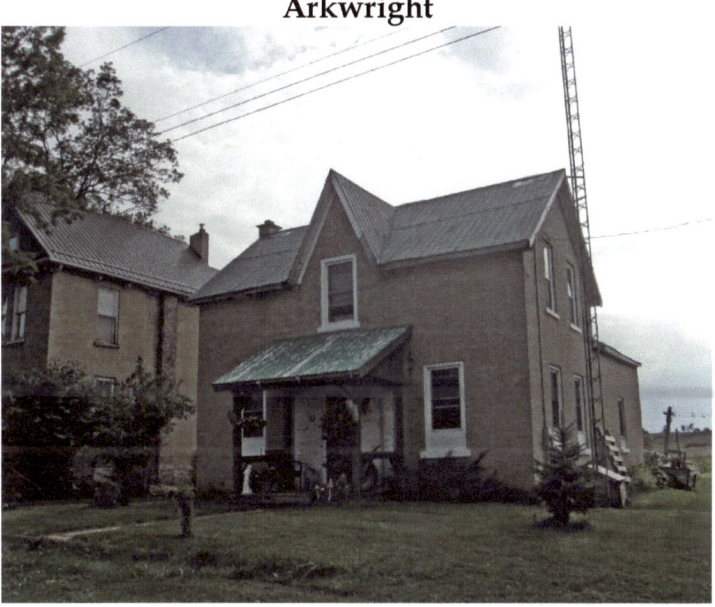

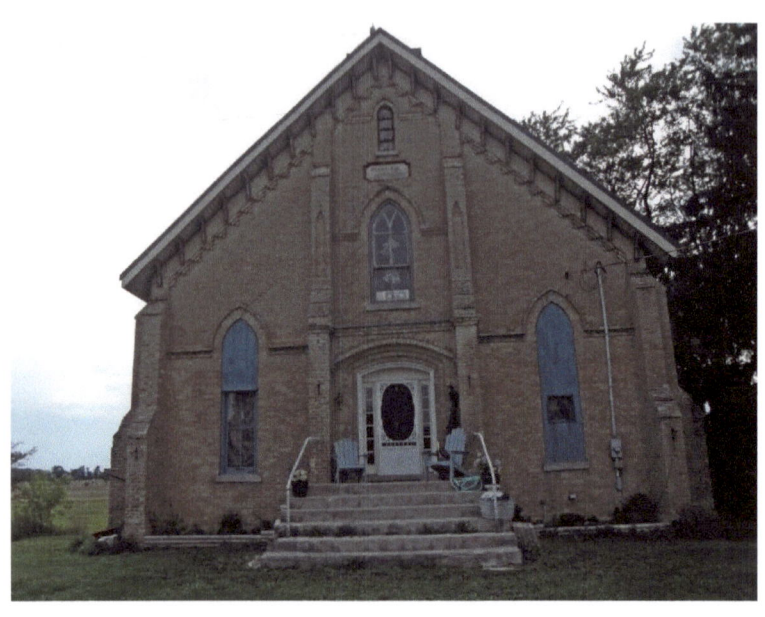

Arkwright United Church – lancet windows, buttresses, dentil molding

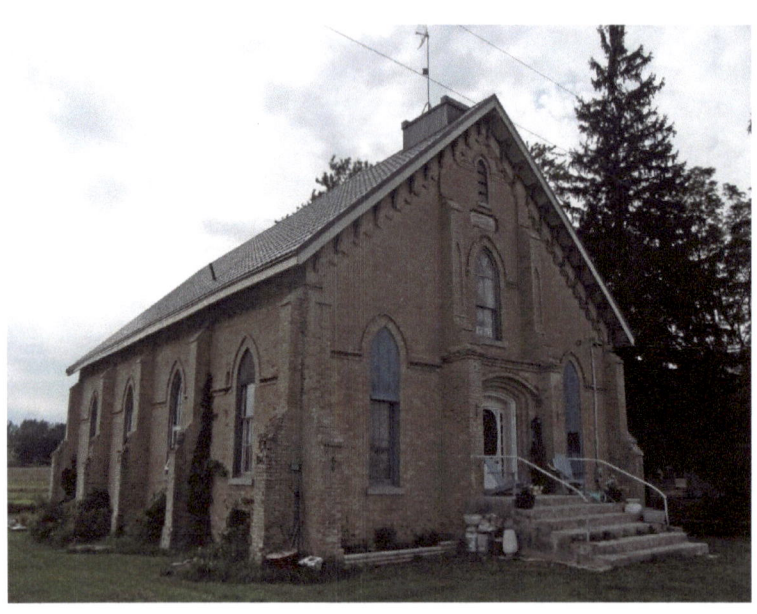

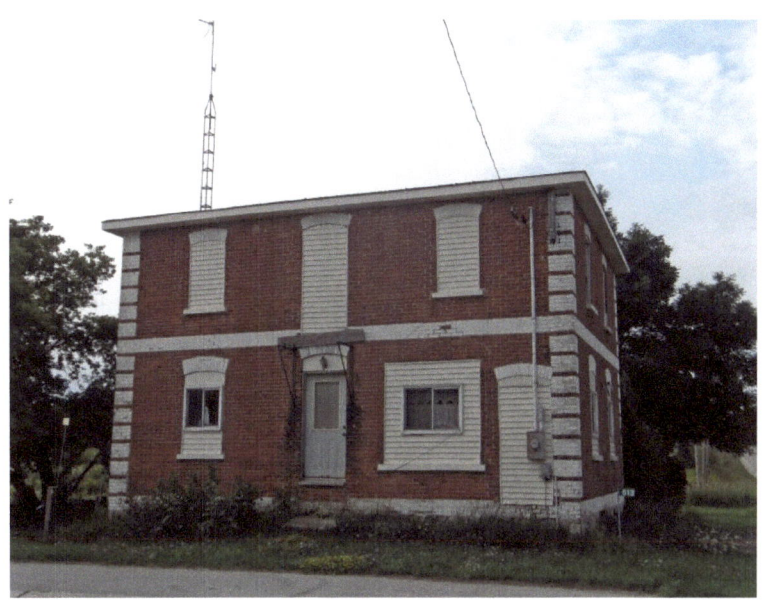

Corner quoins

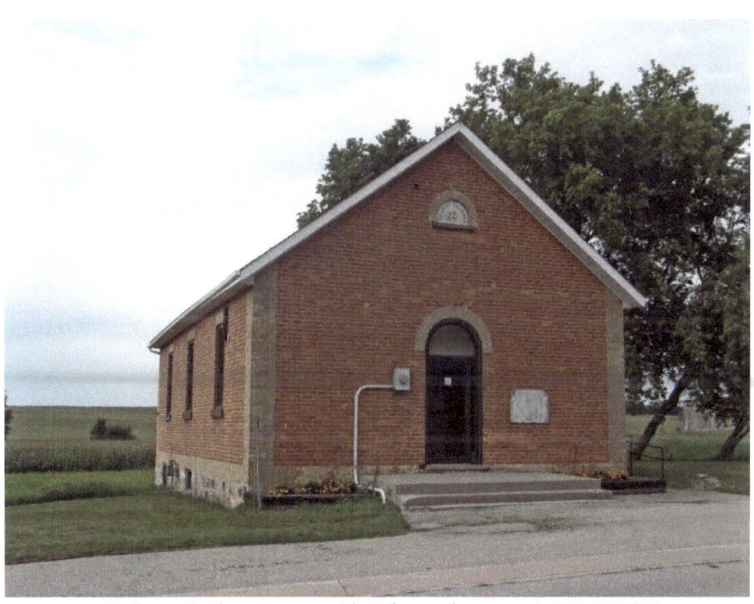

Arkwright Council Chamber – A.D. 1895

Dobbinton

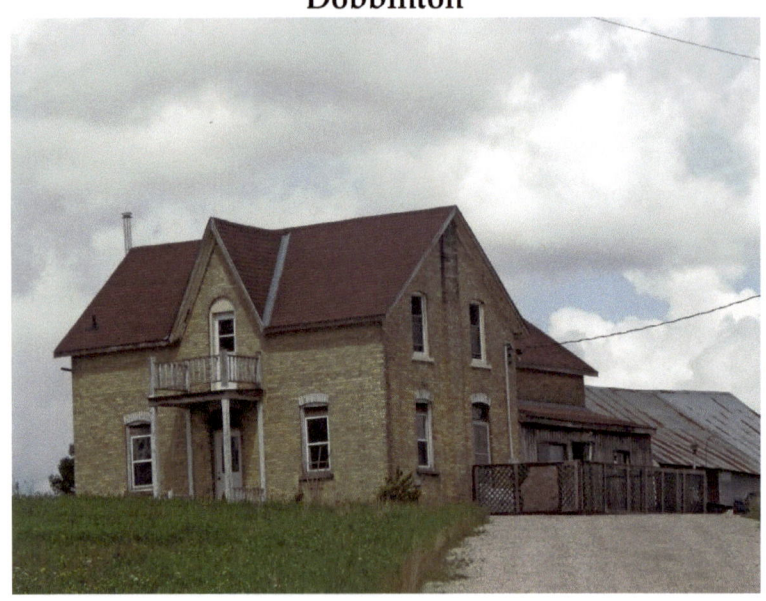

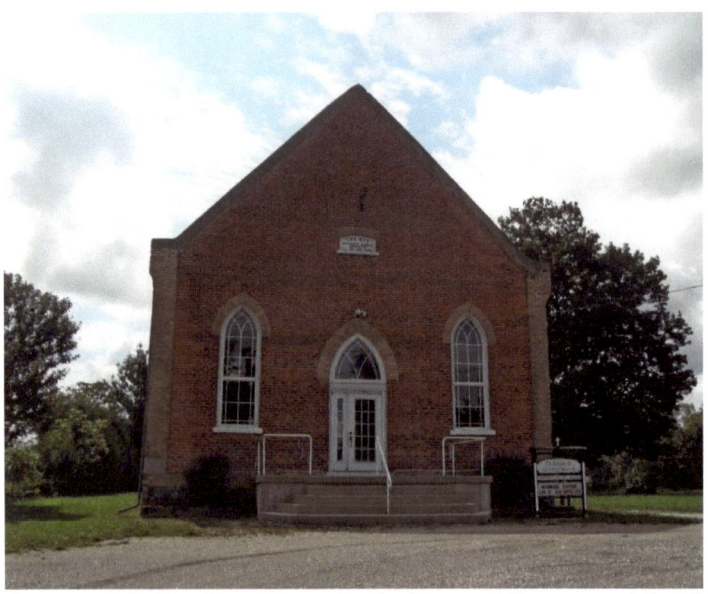

Dobbinton Methodist Church dedicated January 29, 1893 – lancet windows

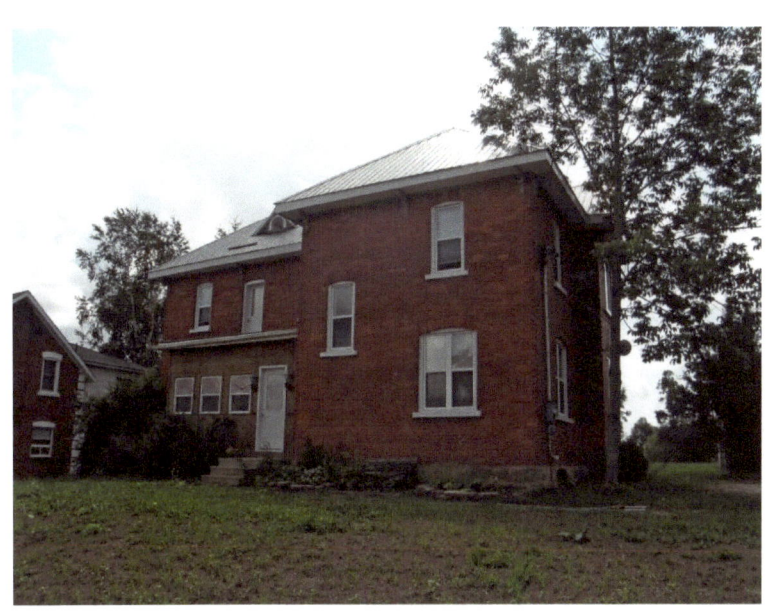

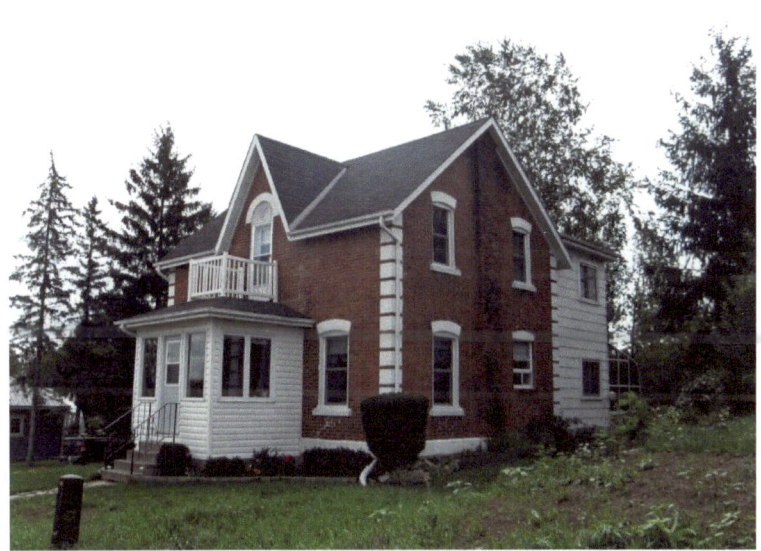

Gothic - corner quoins

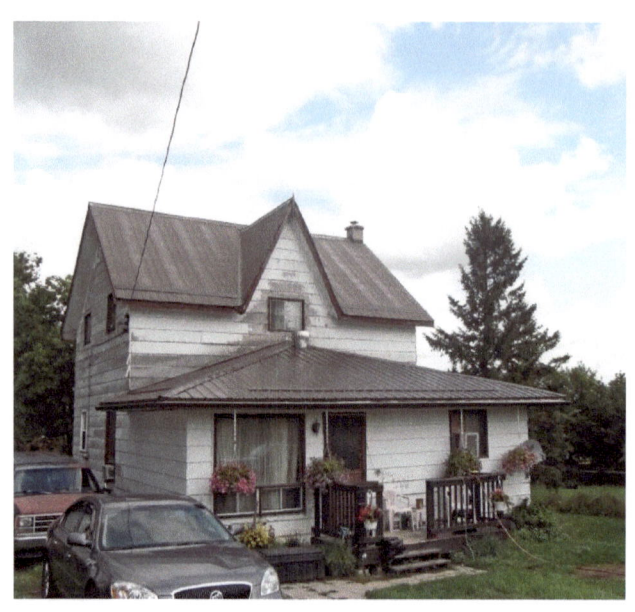

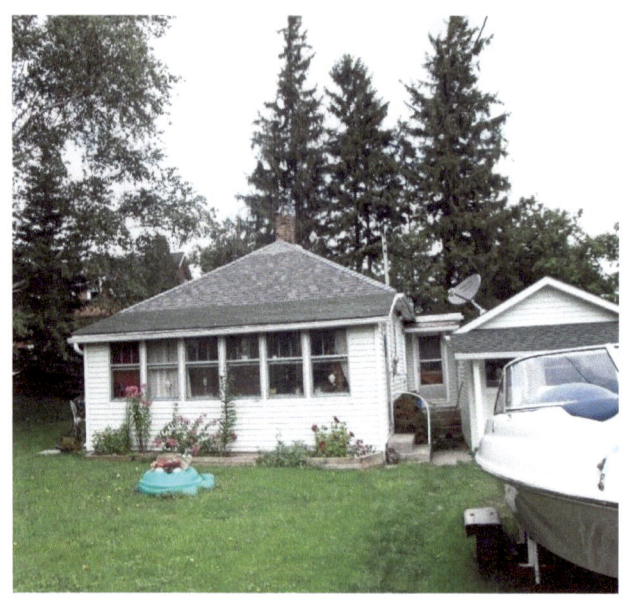

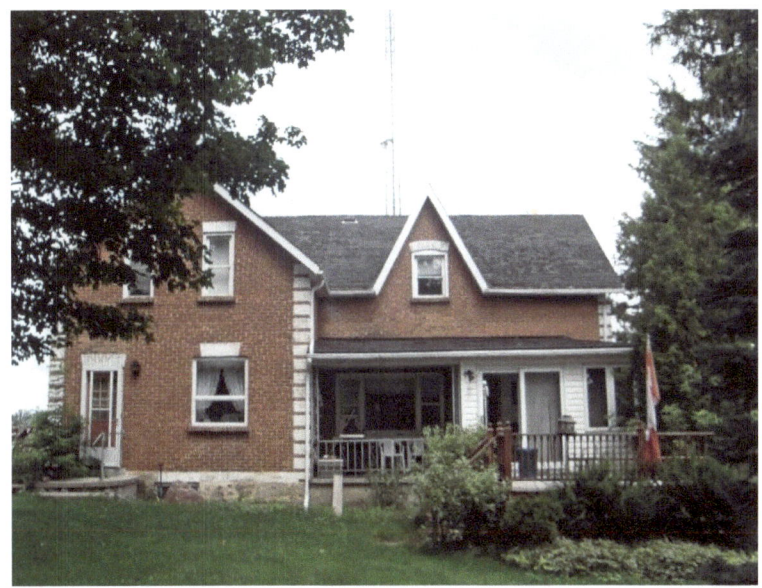

Gothic

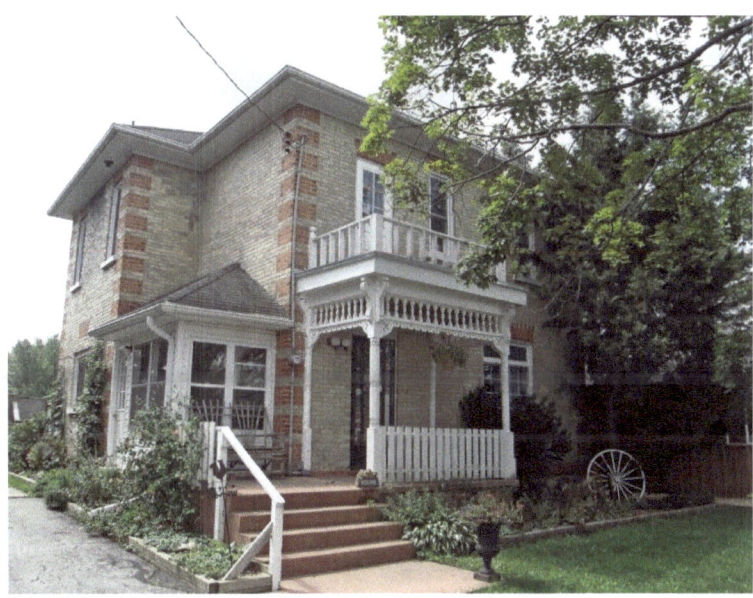

Corner quoins, second floor balcony, spindles on veranda

Tara

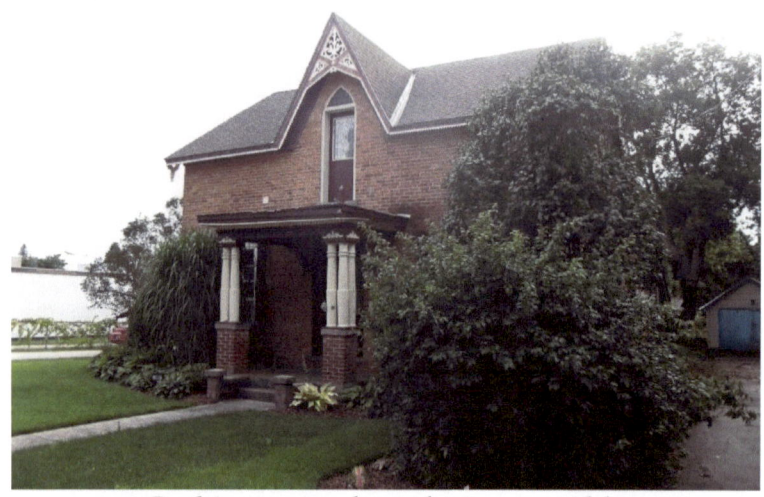

Gothic – verge board trim on gable

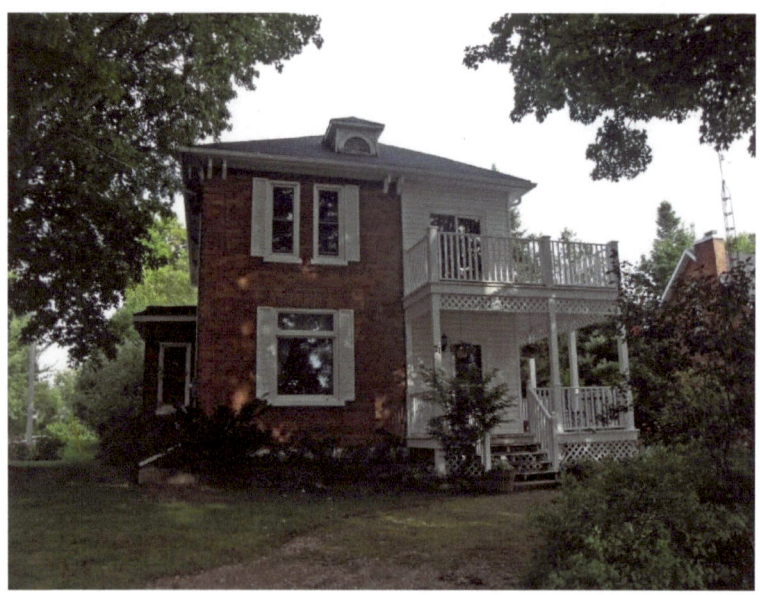

Hipped roof with dormer, cornice brackets

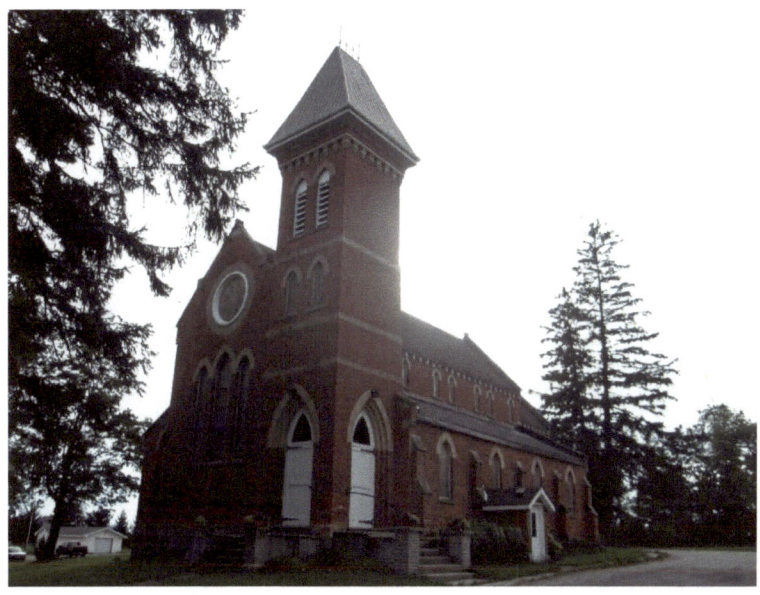

Tara Christ Church Anglican – established 1877 – lancet windows, rose window, buttresses, three-storey tower

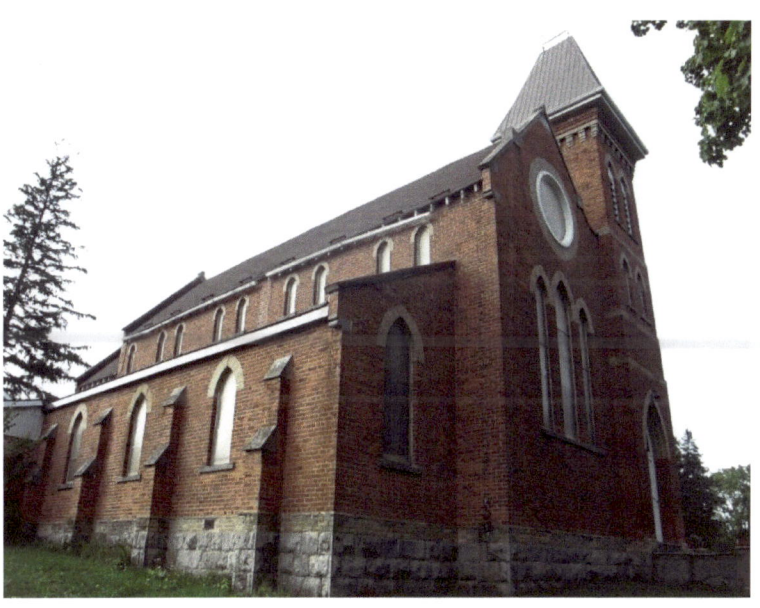

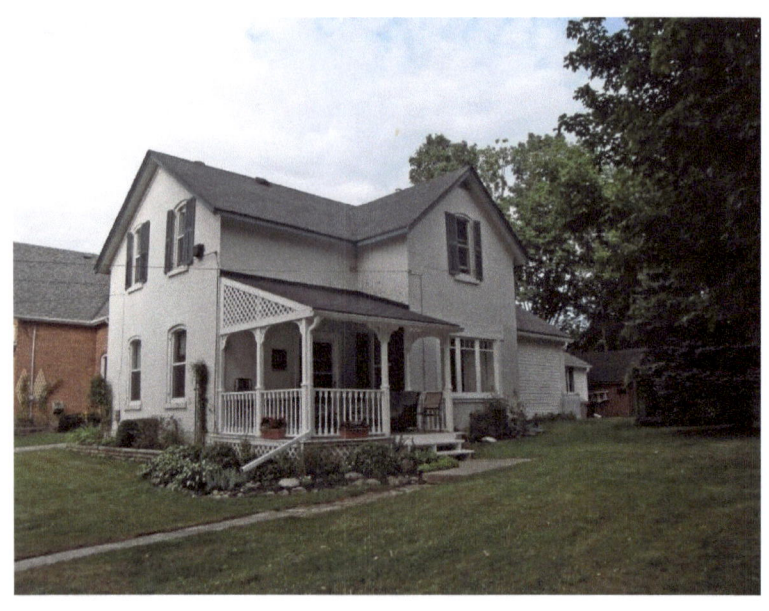

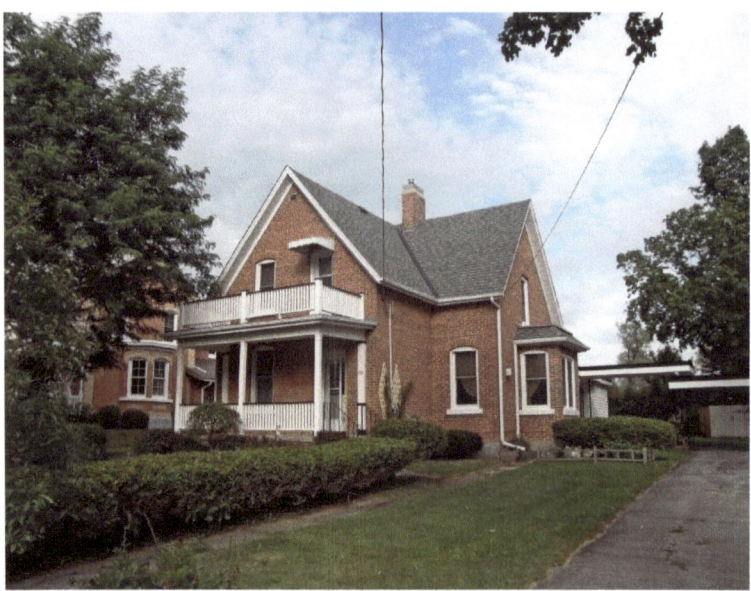

Bay window

Tara

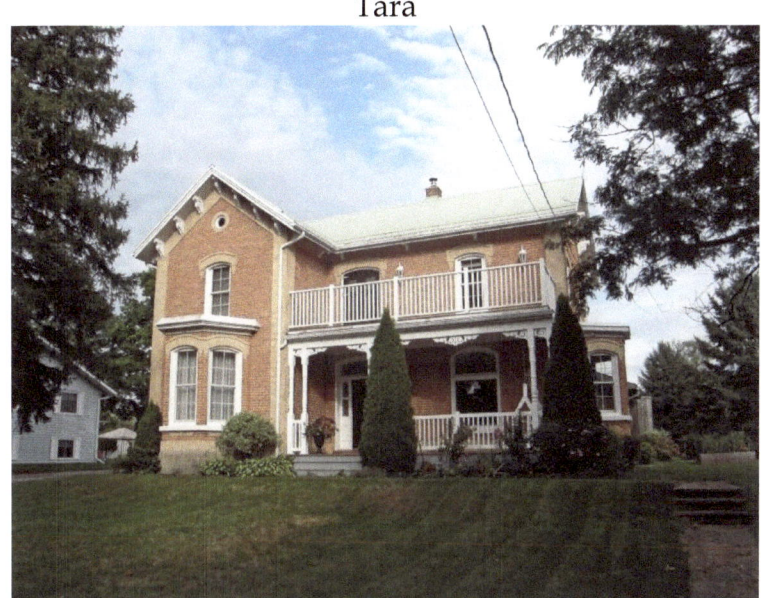

Bay window

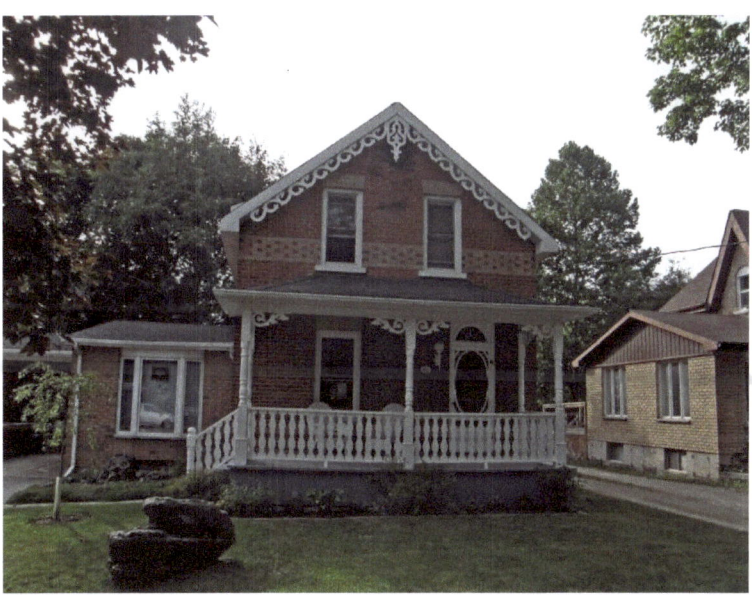

Verge board trim and finial on gable, dichromatic banding

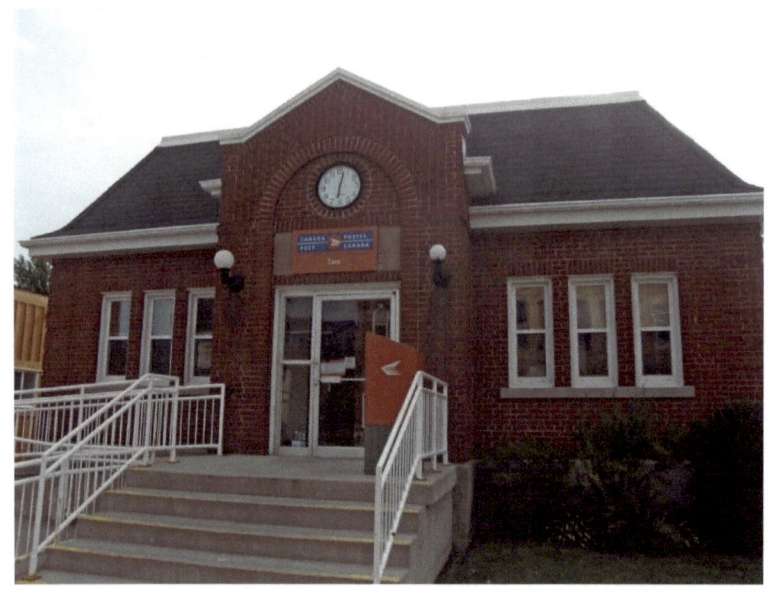

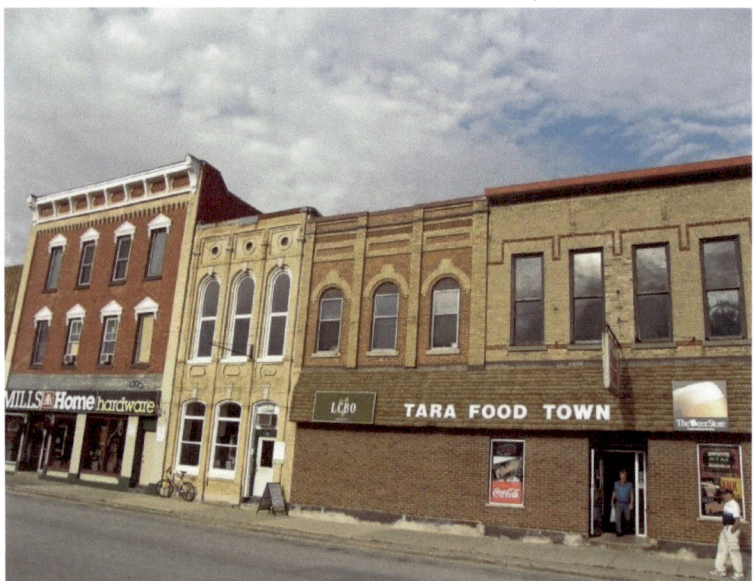

Pilasters, voussoirs and keystones

Tara

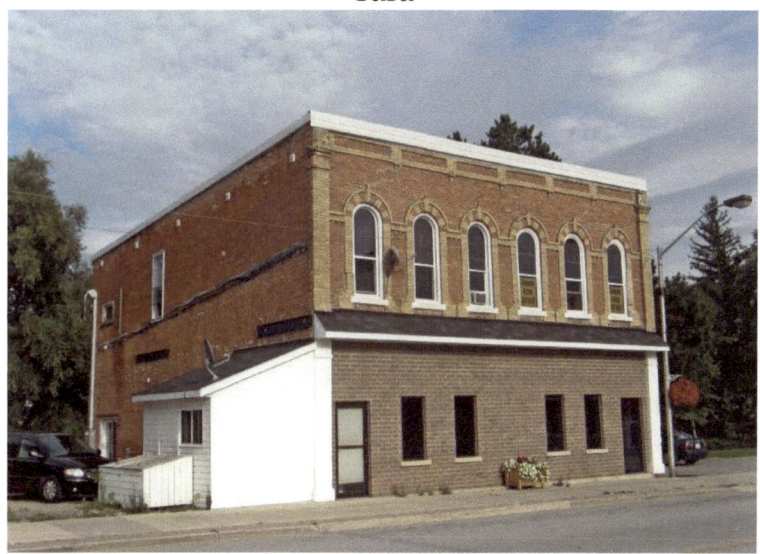

Dichromatic brickwork – voussoirs and keystones

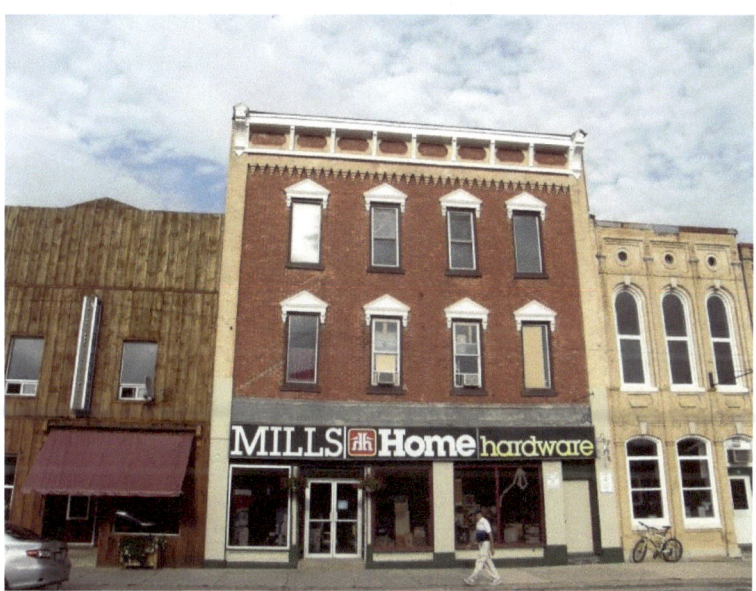

Decorative cornice, beveled dentil molding, triangular window hoods

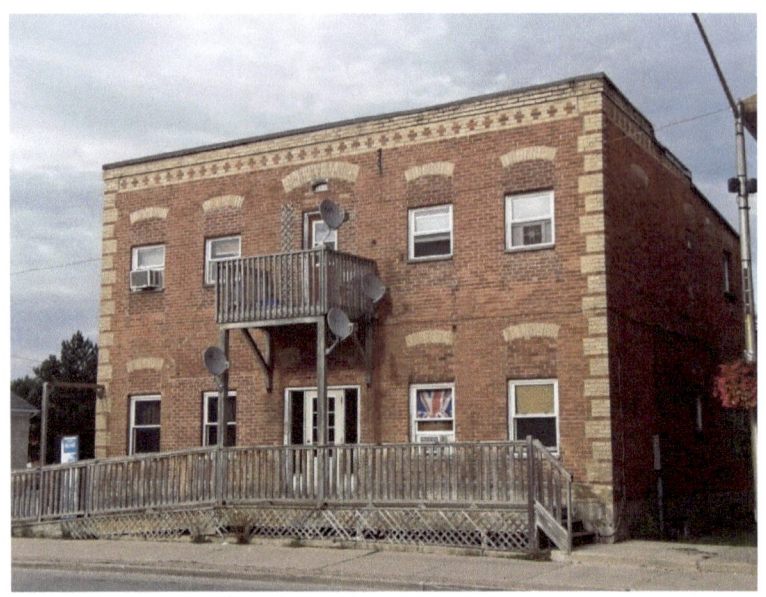

Dichromatic brickwork, corner quoins, voussoirs

Williscroft

Baptist Church – lancet windows with stained glass

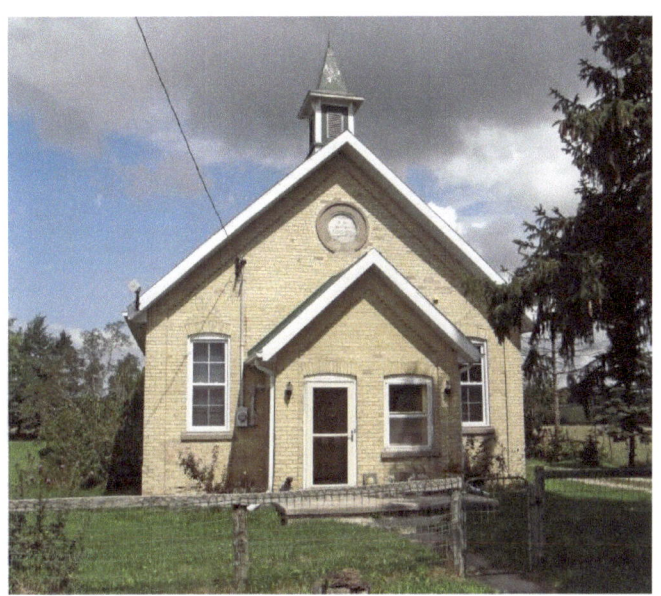

S.S. No. 8 Elderslie school – 1907

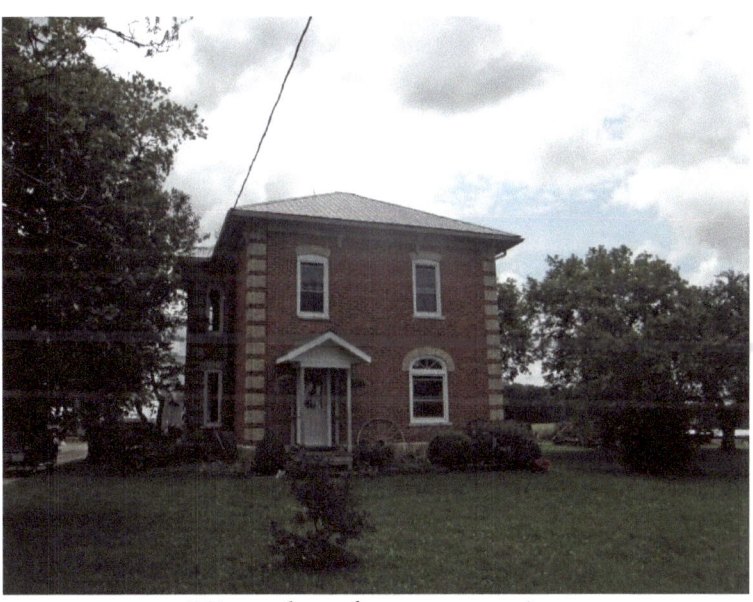

Hipped roof, corner quoins

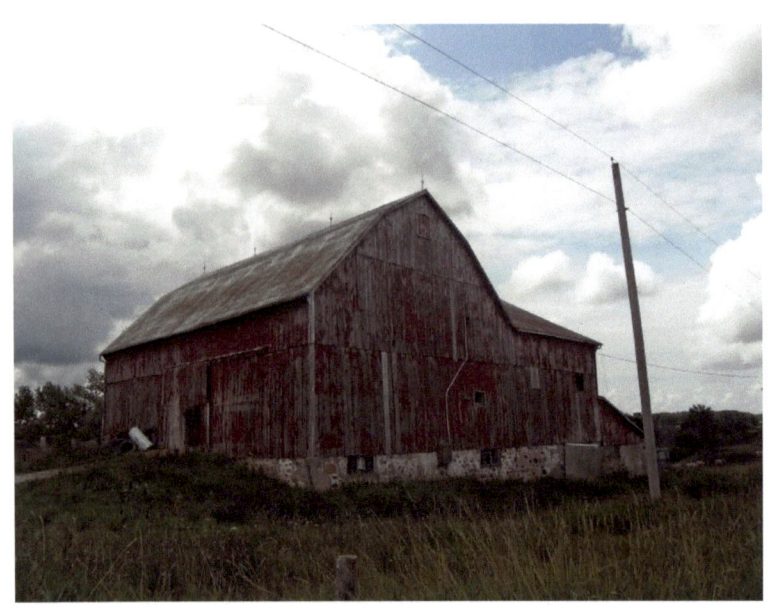

Barns

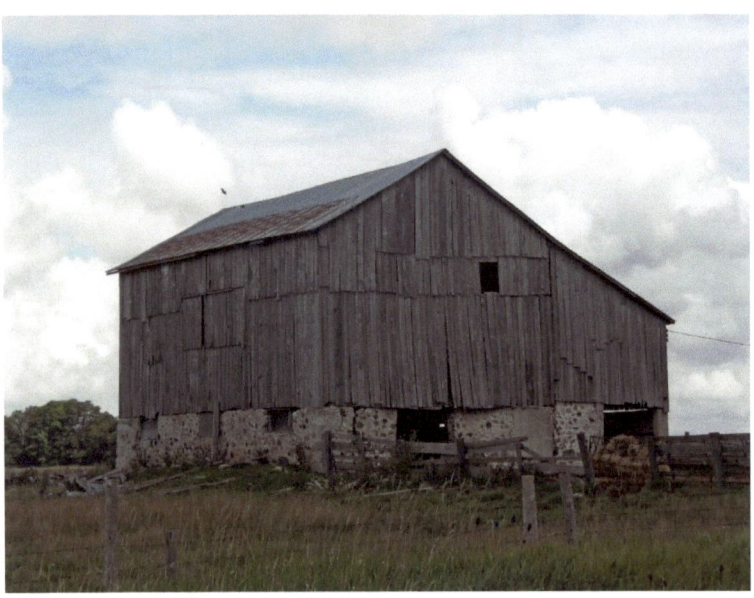

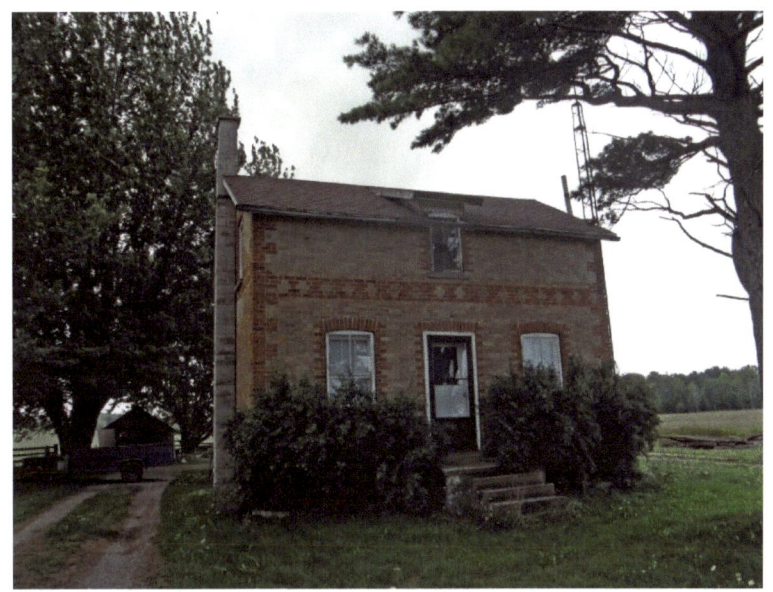

Dichromatic brickwork and banding

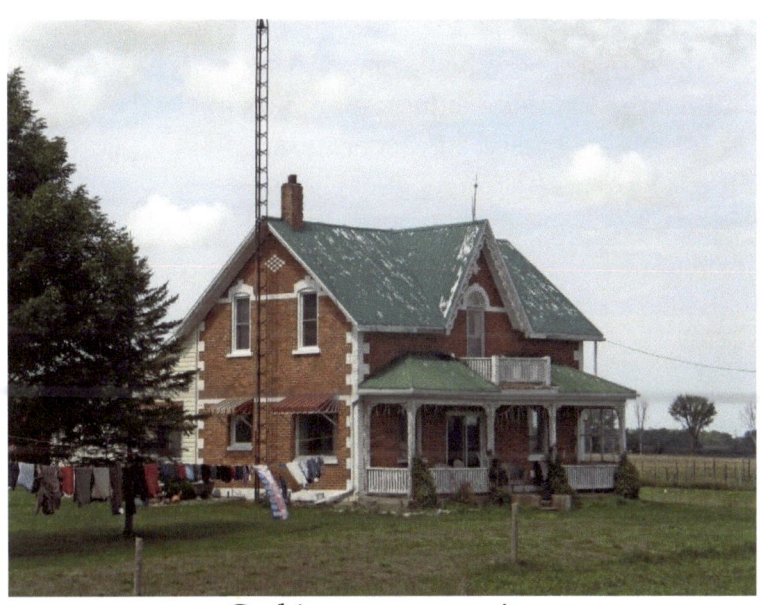

Gothic – corner quoins

Architectural Terms

Banding: Different materials, colors or textures used in horizontal bands along a wall. Example: 777346 Ontario 10, Chatsworth, Page 11	
Battlement: A design for a parapet that has alternating solid parts and openings, originally used for defense, but later used as a decorative motif. Example: Chalmers United Church, Keady, Page 37	
Bay Window: A window that projects out from a wall, in a semicircular, rectangular, or polygonal design. Used frequently in Gothic and Victorian designs. Example: Desboro, Page 18	
Buttress: a masonry structure built against or projecting from a wall which serves to support or reinforce the wall. In Canadian architecture, they are sometimes used for decoration. Example: 43 Toronto Street, Chatsworth, Page 14	
Dichromatic brickwork: the use of two colours of brick, tile or slate to decorate a façade. Example: Desboro, Page 18	
Dormer: (French for "sleep") a gable end window that pierces through the plane of a sloping roof surface to create usable space in the top floor or attic of a building by adding headroom. Example: #136168, Desboro, Page 24	

Gable: the triangular portion of a wall between the edges of a sloping roof. Example: Desboro, Page 17	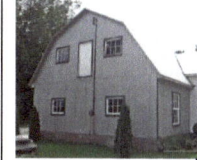
Gambrel Roof: a symmetrical two-sided roof with two slopes on each side; the upper slope is positioned at a shallow angle, while the lower slope is steep. It is similar to a mansard roof, but a gambrel has vertical gable ends instead of being hipped at the four corners of the building. Example: Desboro, Page 28	
Hipped Roof: a roof where all sides slope downwards to the walls with no gables. Example: #136168, Desboro, Page 24	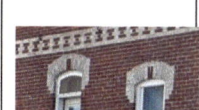
Keystones and Voussoirs: a voussoir is a wedge-shaped element used in building an arch. A keystone is the central stone that locks all the stones into position, allowing the arch to bear weight. A keystone is often enlarged and embellished. Example: Grey Road 40 and Grey Road 3, Page 32	
Lancet Window: a tall, narrow window with a pointed arch at its top. Example: 22 John Street, Chatsworth, Page 15	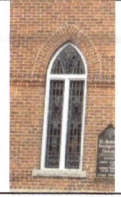

Pilaster: a slightly projecting column built into or applied to the face of a wall for additional structural support. Example: 271 Garafraxa Street, Chatsworth, Page 12	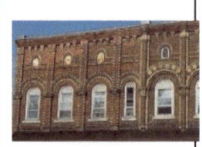
Quoin: masonry blocks at the corner of a wall, often a decorative feature, usually larger or of a different colour than the rest of the wall. Example: Williamsford, Page 34	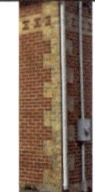
Rose Window: a circular window with ornamental tracery radiating from the centre. Example: 22 John Street, Chatsworth, Page 15	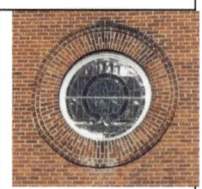
Tower: A circular, square, or octagonal vertical structure higher than the surrounding structure that is usually part of an existing building and is created either for extra defense or for a specific purpose such as a clock or a bell tower. Example: Latona Presbyterian Church, Dornoch, Page 29	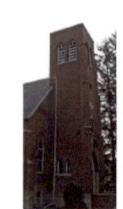
Verge board and Finial: also called bargeboards – hang from the projecting end of a roof and are often elaborately carved and ornamented. **Finial:** ornament added to the top of a gable, pinnacle, canopy or spire – a Gothic element. Example: Desboro, Page 21	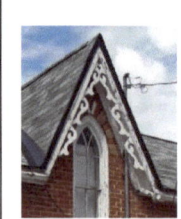

Building Styles

Edwardian, 1900-1930 – This style bridges the ornate and elaborate styles of the Victorian era and the simplified styles of the 20th century. Edwardian Classicism provided simple, balanced facades, simple rooflines, dormer windows, large front porches, and smooth brick surfaces. Voussoirs and keystones are used sparingly and are understated. Finials and cresting are absent. Cornice brackets and braces are block-like and openings have flat arches or plain stone lintels. Example: Chatsworth, Page 15	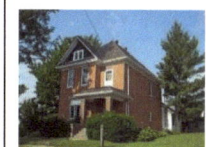
Gothic Revival, 1830-1890 – These decorative buildings have sharply-pitched gables with highly detailed verge boards, pointed-arch window openings, and dichromatic brickwork. It is a common style in Ontario. Example: #141, Chatsworth, Page 11	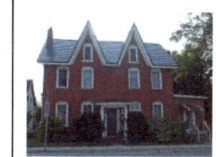
Italianate, 1850-1900 – A two story rectangular building with a mild hip roof, a projecting frontispiece, and generous eaves with ornate cornice brackets was the basis of the style; often there are large sash windows, quoins, ornate detailing on the windows, belvederes and wraparound verandahs. Italianate commercial buildings often have cast iron cresting and elegant window surrounds. Example: Desboro, Page 24	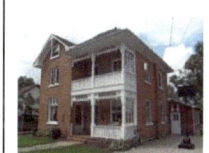

A **log cabin**, built from logs, was usually one- or 1½-storeys constructed with round rather than hewn, or hand-worked, logs, and erected quickly for frontier shelter. Log cabins were built from logs laid horizontally and interlocked on the ends with notches. The cabin was situated to provide sunlight and drainage so the pioneers could cope better with the rigors of frontier life. The pioneers chose old-growth trees that were straight and had few knots and did not need to be hewn to fit well together. Careful notching minimized the size of the gap between the logs and reduced the amount of chinking with sticks and rocks or daubing with mud to fill the gap. The length of one log was the length of one wall. Example: Grey Road 40 and Grey Road 3, Page 32	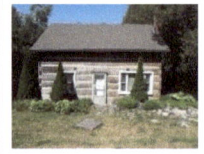
Regency Cottage, 1830-1860 – This style originated in England in 1815 and spread to Ontario later in the 19th century as British officers retired to Canada. It is a modest one-storey house with a low-pitched hip roof and has a symmetrical front façade. Example: Desboro, Page 23	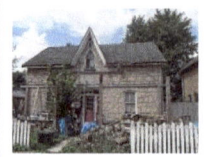

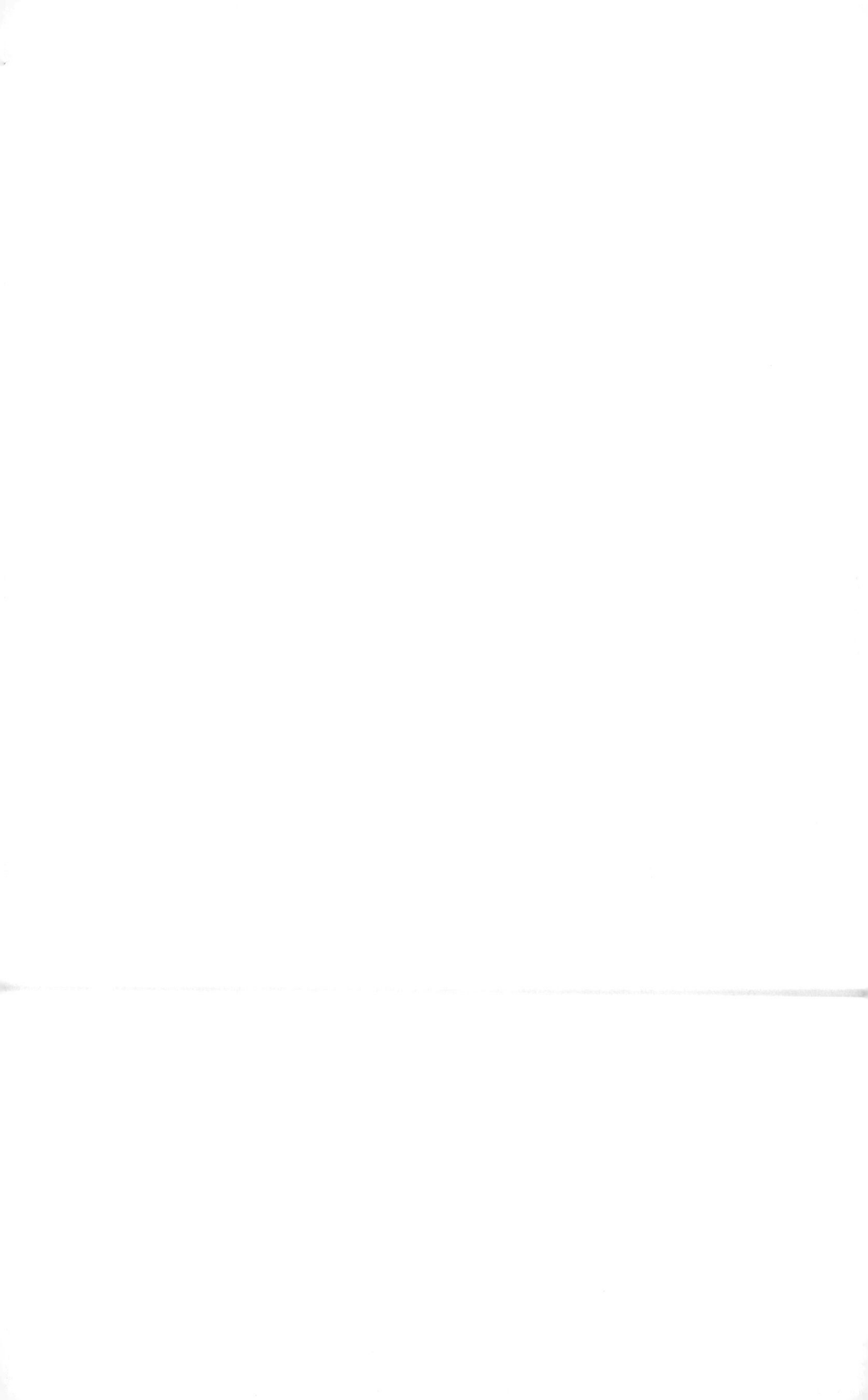

www.ingramcontent.com/pod-product-compliance
Lightning Source LLC
Chambersburg PA
CBHW041941240526
45473CB00033B/182